Making It
BETTER

Making It BETTER

Activities for Children Living in a Stressful World

SECOND EDITION

Barbara Oehlberg

Redleaf Press®
www.redleafpress.org
800-423-8309

Published by Redleaf Press
10 Yorkton Court
St. Paul, MN 55117
www.redleafpress.org

First edition published 1996. Second edition 2014.
Cover design by Jim Handrigan
Cover photographs/illustrations by Stephanie Roth
Interior design by 4 Seasons Book Design/Michelle Cook and typeset in Rotis Serif.
Interior photos/illustrations by Stephanie Roth
Printed in the United States of America
20 19 18 17 16 15 14 13   1 2 3 4 5 6 7 8

Library of Congress Cataloging-in-Publication Data
Oehlberg, Barbara, 1932-
   Making it better : activities for children living in a stressful world / Barbara Oehlberg. — Second edition.
      pages cm.
      Summary: "This second edition speaks to the concept of 'trauma-informed' early childhood education and includes many activities to help fragile children process and heal from stressful events, including natural disasters, community and family violence, extensive medical treatments, complicated family dynamics, deployment of a parent in the military, and more" — Provided by publisher.
   Includes bibliographical references.
   ISBN 978-1-60554-160-0 (pbk.)
   1. Early childhood education—Activity programs. 2. Stress in children. 3. Stress management for children. 4. Grief in children. 5. School psychology.   I. Title.
   LB1139.35.A37O44 2013
   372.21—dc23
                                    2013031583

Printed on acid-free paper

This book is dedicated to
Mallory Floyd, Susan Ross,
and Vanessa Stergios,
the three dedicated women
who made the
"Growing the Brain" project
become a reality at
Belden Elementary School,
Canton, Ohio,
and to our grandchildren.

Children

Children
Children are the promise of the future
Children are the vessel containing all the incidents and events of their
    family, generation upon generation
Children, who often force us to face our values in spite of ourselves.

Children
Children, the insistent voice of what might have been, what could
    have happened differently in their family system, their community
Children, the eternal voice of fairness and justice
Children, the ones who insistently demand our best, in spite of the
    consequences to themselves.

Children
Children, who have the right to experience dignity and respect
Children, who instead are referred to by what they are rather than
    who they are
Children, referred to as that ADHD kid, the behavior-problem child,
    the bully.

Children
Children, who are ignored because they are not able to meet our
    expectations
Children, who just want attention because they need attention
Children, who are shunned because they are daydreamers, shy, or
    withdrawn.

Children
Children, who talk back and act out
Children, who melt down into total tantrums in shopping malls
Children, who show us over and over that they feel insecure and
    stressed but are considered misbehaving and reacted to with
    rejection and isolation.

Children

Children, who are exploited by a materialistic society

Children, valued more as future consumers than for the creative
potential they embody

Children, who are considered belonging to their parents rather than
individuals in their own right

Children, who are expected to become the child their parents want
them to be instead of who they were created to be.

Children

Children, who are considered disrespectful when they express righteous
anger

Children, who are expected to be nice and make adults look good

Children, who are virtually voiceless in our democracy because they
cannot vote

Children, who are presumed not to have the same rights as adults.

Children

Children, who will eventually shape our society and become its leaders

Children, who are all born with promise and creativity

Children, who will become adults filled with hope or disdain, depending
on how they experienced childhood

Children, who will take care of us when we are frail and elderly, in
the same way we treated them when they were children.

—Barbara Oehlberg

Contents

Introduction to Trauma-Informed Early Childhood Education . . . 1

Part One: Childhood Changed: Understanding Trauma 5

Chapter 1: Attachment and the Growing Brain 9

Chapter 2: Early Traumatic Stress 17

Chapter 3: Implementing the Trauma-Informed Classroom . . 29

Chapter 4: Trauma-Informed Discipline 37

Chapter 5: The Unique Grieving Process for Each Child . . . 47

Chapter 6: Helping Children Build Resiliency 61

Part Two: Classroom Activities for Empowerment 69

Chapter 7: Healing Play 75

Chapter 8: Healing Arts 105

Chapter 9: Healing Language Arts 165

Appendix A: Making Referrals 195

Appendix B: Resources 198

Appendix C: Index of Activities by Issue 203

References 212

Introduction to Trauma-Informed Early Childhood Education

Teachers everywhere have struggled as they work with children and try to understand children's behaviors, particularly in the past several years. Children have not changed. Childhood has, and the children in today's classrooms merely reflect the challenging, sometimes scary changes in their environments and world.

The Brain and Education

As neurologists learn more about childhood and brain development, a growing body of research has established the importance of supporting children through the toughest kinds of childhoods. Many students come from backgrounds and life experiences that don't align with status quo educational pedagogy. Educators must find new approaches to students' learning and developmental needs, even if these require significant changes in traditional approaches to discipline and student learning. It has become very apparent that adapting to these students' needs will require a major paradigm shift in education, from birth to high school. Even what are understood to be developmentally appropriate practices will need to be scrutinized. This educational shift must involve the infusion of practices and policies that meet the emotional and learning needs of children of all ages.

The original edition of *Making It Better* was published in 1996, when neurological research had just begun to be reported. This growing body of research immediately resonated with me as a light of hope and insight into the national dilemma of poor achievement and behavioral issues. In recent years, it has proven to be exactly that.

This revised edition of *Making It Better* is designed to help educators create safe, nurturing environments for their students based on an understanding of foundational neurological principles and theories. Early child educators have always tried to "do no harm." Dedicated educators know that while providing lots of love is a major requirement of early childhood teachers, nurturing today's children can look significantly different than it did thirty or forty years ago. In today's world, distressed children need absolute emotional security and an opportunity to engage in healing activities.

Trauma-Informed Education

Trauma-informed education is an approach discussed in this book that responds to the learning and behavioral needs of children who have experienced traumatic events or toxic stress (a repeated stressful experience with long-term negative effects). Trauma-informed early childhood education applies neurological research to teaching, disciplinary policies, and school climate issues.

The following are reasons for incorporating trauma-informed education:

- to maximize students' sense of security, both emotional and physical
- to strengthen students' self-regulation skills
- to accommodate the emotional needs of stressed and anxious students
- to promote a supportive and cooperative school climate
- to reduce student aggression, conflicts, and bullying behaviors
- to enhance the development of empathy in students
- to elevate student achievement
- to provide an environment in which every child can reach his full potential
- to increase teachers' satisfaction in their professional role
- to generate a sense of hope for the future in all students

Trauma-informed teaching is not a critique of what was prescribed in the past. It is a research-based approach that can make teaching more enjoyable and enhance academic achievement. Most importantly, it lights a path to a brighter future for the children we teach. Children living with uncertainty and insecurity may have great difficulty focusing on learning. You may be the anchor needed to make sense out of their world. The opportunity to make a difference in children's lives has never been greater than it is today with trauma-informed education. For some students, you may provide the only supportive relationship in their lives, helping them begin to develop their full potential.

Using the Activities

The heart of this book is a collection of group activities and personal strategies that make it possible for children to engage in self-healing and self-empowerment. These activities will enrich the learning process and help all students learn more deeply. Through this process, they can integrate their life experiences into their learning and begin to make sense out of a world that often seems threatening. My sincere goal is that through the recommendations of this book, both you and the children you teach and care for will find renewed hope and delight as together we embrace the future.

One caution to note: The activities in this book are not intended to place teachers in a counselor's or therapist's role. Some children may need to be referred for assessment or individual counseling following the use of these activities if the behavioral issues do not subside. The activities in this book are never to be used in place of mandated reporting of suspected child abuse or neglect.

PART ONE

Childhood Changed: Understanding Trauma

It is Monday morning, fifteen minutes into class, and already Brian and James, two second graders in a city school, have been out of their seats three times, bickering and posturing, finally ending with a scuffle on the floor. Another week of classroom disarray begins. Another committed teacher is frustrated and dismayed, aware that the performance test scores for this class are falling, not progressing. In a small town halfway across the country, Jenny and Andre, two four-year-olds, are swearing and exchanging obscene gestures at their child care center. The staff shake their heads and wonder if there are any sweet, cute kids anywhere.

Incidents like these are repeated across the nation from urban centers to rural communities. Impulsive student aggressiveness is escalating while test scores are plummeting. Are these two realities interconnected? And more importantly, why is this happening now in your school, center, or home?

The reasons are multiple and complex. Children in the United States are growing up in a culture where violence is glamorized in entertainment and sports. Changes in family structure and mobility can lead to a loss of connectedness with relatives and supportive adults in children's lives. The number of children living in poverty has increased in the past decade, and it is not uncommon for children to witness violence within their homes or on the streets that surround them.

Throughout history, children have witnessed frightening events as a result of natural disasters or human activities. Many recovered successfully and have moved on to have happy and healthy lives. What is different today is the combined effects of societal changes in both family and community. Families work, play, and eat differently from their ancestors. Children are repeatedly exposed to real and fictional violent acts on the TV screens in their living rooms. These experiences—and many others—affect both children's and adults' brain development.

Young children are particularly vulnerable to the effects of violence. Children who witness family violence may never feel safe unless they receive support from caring adults. Without support, children exposed to familial violence experience persistent or "toxic" stress, which has lifelong effects. Powerlessness and terror may be prevailing feelings, even during "stable" periods. But how does this connect with the acting-out behavior of Brian and James or Jenny and Andre on Monday morning?

According to developing research in the field, children who demonstrate disrespectful and belligerent behaviors in school or other group settings often do so as a result of their altered brain development caused by certain high-stress life experiences. As inappropriate as acting-out behaviors are, in trauma-informed teaching, you can interpret such aggressiveness as a child's pleading for an opportunity to feel safe, physically and emotionally. The angry, raging child may actually be a very frightened child. The defiant child is crying out for stability and a sense of security. As educators work to help distressed and traumatized children learn in the midst of chaos, they can be part of children's lifelong healing and recovery.

1. Attachment and the Growing Brain

In an elementary school for which I provided an after-school staff development session, the kindergarten teacher had a private question as we left. She was unsure of the way her aide had dealt with a situation earlier that afternoon.

A boy, frequently at the center of a troubling eruption, had aggressively forced his way into a small group playing quietly in the block area. When they resisted his intrusion, he threw a block at them and knocked down their creation.

The aide snatched him away and chided his actions. She sternly made him sit at an empty table off to the side, where he cried and fussed loudly.

When the lead teacher returned to the room upon hearing the wailing and learned of the situation, she wondered if this was the answer to his poor social skills, because it happened every day, sometimes twice. I suggested we ask ourselves what might be at the base of his limited social skills. I reminded her that children who had weak attachments missed out on the neuro wiring that allowed them to develop relationships and the skills to build friendships. Understanding that, what might we do to strengthen his skills, and would being isolated help? Might he be interpreting being isolated as a rejection?

The next day when he had a meltdown, his teacher knelt down to eye level, slowly took one of his hands in hers, and asked, "What would you like to see happen so you can feel a part of the group? How might I help you with that?" He replied, "Just walk over to the table with me and stand there." There were very few incidents after that.

Sometimes children's behavior is baffling and doesn't fit into past models. How can educators understand and respond to these upsetting behaviors? Two concepts that can help explain some children's extreme behavior are brain development and attachment theory.

Growing the Brain

One basic principle is that the brain develops based on the experiences it has—sights, sounds, tastes, smells, textures—which actually create neural structures that give meaning to the world based on those experiences. A useful picture is that the brain is like a field with paths being built across it. As the brain tries to make sense of the world around it, a neural pathway is built, step-by-step, every time the brain needs to perform a new action or explain a new event. The brain continues to travel the paths until they are well-worn ruts, which makes them even easier to travel again and again. The more a particular neurological pathway or pattern is traveled, the more it is established, trampled down, and used again and again. The less a route is used, the more it gets "overgrown" or ignored. In this way, for example, an initially complex task like tying shoelaces becomes automatic: the neural pathways for shoelace tying are established for quick usage. A newborn baby is constantly building and rebuilding many thousands of new neural pathways; this building process continues in stages and growth spurts throughout childhood, slowing significantly into adulthood.

How do these ideas of brain development apply to early childhood behavior? It means that a child who has experienced secure and stable relationships in a loving environment will approach the rest of the world with that continued expectation, as he or she continues to travel the pathways that are already built. And a child who has experienced a chaotic or abusive environment will respond to the rest of the world as though it will be chaotic or abusive, because those are the pathways that have been traveled for months or years. Building new paths is possible, but it takes time, patience, and repetition for those pathways to stick.

A second principle is that the brain develops in a "hierarchical" pattern, meaning that less complex brain structures develop first before more complex brain structures. This means that as an infant is developing a coherent understanding of the world, early experiences may be imprinted in the "earlier" parts of the brain—responsible for things like regulating heart rate or emotional response—long before the higher-level parts of the brain—areas that involve abstract thought or logical reasoning—are fully capable of processing them. Just because a child does not remember an experience is no guarantee that it did not affect him or her. Sometimes a reaction to a specific situation can be a result of the brain functioning based on early neural pathways developed by that early, unremembered experience (Cozolino 2006; Schore 2003). These "implicit" memories can be particularly frightening for infants and toddlers who have witnessed or heard the sounds of domestic violence but are unable to talk about it (Perry and Szalavitz 2006). Who hasn't heard an adult claim he or she was thankful an infant or toddler was spared the terror of an experience or event because she or he was too young to consciously remember it? Yet that child may have never been helped to understand the event, which some part of the brain does remember. Try as we may, we really can never convince a child to simply forget troubling events, because our words have little impact on the memory as it was absorbed and recorded in the developing brain (Perry 2004). While caregivers and educators may not be able to question children about these experiences, understanding how the brain works can be useful in knowing how to help children move forward and forge new behavioral and thinking patterns to follow.

Attachment: It's a Way of Life

Another impact on children's behavior is the strength and quality of their earliest relationships with their first caregivers, usually their parents. *Attachment theory* is a way of explaining how people negotiate relationships based on their earliest experiences with primary caregivers. In its most basic form, attachment theory says that a child's very early relationships with parents or other primary caregivers will shape the way that child will interact in future relationships. The theory was developed in the years following World War II by psychologist John Bowlby as a result of his work with many disruptive or struggling children who had been orphaned or otherwise traumatized during the war. Bowlby and his student Mary Ainsworth developed a model that explained how children create very early "attachment relationships" with their primary caregivers. One famous attachment study by Tronick and colleagues (1978) involved mothers who would suddenly become unresponsive and expressionless toward their infants for a period of time (called the "still face experiment"); based on the infant's response to this sudden withdrawal and then the mother's resumed interaction, researchers identified the infant's "attachment style"; that is, the infant's response showed what the infant *already expected* from the mother's interaction based on previous experience. While infants with secure attachments naturally became distressed by the unusual interaction, others with insecure attachment styles appeared to expect inconsistent interaction or to be ignored completely. This study and earlier research by Ainsworth are the basis for attachment theory.

- **Secure attachment** describes the attachment style of a child who sees the caregiver as a "secure base" from which to explore and also return to for comfort, based on a caregiver who is available, responsive, and consistently supportive. This child is better able to balance his emotions, create meaningful relationships, and securely handle stress as his brain develops.

- **Insecure avoidant attachment** describes the style of a child who tries to avoid dependence on other relationships for support, based on a caregiver who is emotionally or physically distant from the child's needs. This child may appear "lost in her own world," or emotionally distant, because she does not expect caregivers to respond to her emotional needs.

- **Insecure ambivalent/resistant attachment** describes the style of a child forming inconsistent relational patterns of emotional clinging and rejection or frustration, based on a caregiver who is also inconsistently supportive or interactive. One example of this type of attachment can be a child who is extremely wary of strangers yet also does not seem to be comforted by his parent's return.

- <u>Insecure disorganized attachment</u> describes the style of a child who tends to fear relationships and may have difficulty regulating or reading emotions, <u>based on a caregiver whose behavior is wildly inconsistent, confusing, frightening, or abusive</u>. A child with this attachment style could, for example, be deeply distressed but choose to lie on the floor and cry (but not just tantrum behavior) rather than to seek comfort from her caregiver in the room, <u>since her fear of being hurt by the caregiver overcomes her need to seek comfort</u>.

Insecure attachments result from the disruption of the relationship between the caregiver and the infant to the extent that a healthy bond does not form. This disruption can be caused by maternal depression, violence toward the infant, inconsistent responses to the infant's needs, or neglect of the infant. <u>Essentially, the child learns that he cannot depend on the caregiver to be responsive to his needs, or worse, he begins to fear the caregiver because of the caregiver's violent or neglectful actions</u>.

Insecure attachment styles and the brain development that accompanies them can contribute to a variety of behavioral and thinking patterns that affect the rest of a person's social and internal life. Current neural research has shed light on the importance of attachment to the development of critical brain circuitry for self-regulation, stress management, and empathy. <u>Children who grow up experiencing secure attachments to their caregiver have stronger self-regulation skills later on</u> (Drake, Belsky, and Fearon 2013). Thus, the care provider's efforts to soothe and comfort fussing infants help build the self-regulation capacity of the child (Cozolino 2006; Cozolino 2013). Similarly, insecure attachments may cause disruptions in the development of areas of the brain responsible for skills such as self-regulation, stress management, and empathy.

Recently, insecure attachment has been linked to possible changes in the brain. Research with adults who had insecure attachments as children has revealed differences in how these adults' brains process social cues and rewarding information compared to adults who had secure attachments (Vrtička and Vuilleumier 2012). Insecure attachments, which may result from relationships with caregivers that are not reciprocal, are disrupted, or are even violent in nature often create situations of toxic stress for the child, resulting in changes in the way the brain interprets incoming information from the environment. <u>These changes may contribute to tendencies of a child to withdraw from or lash out at others around him</u>.

These changes in the brain, though not fully understood, may be linked to later behavioral and learning problems in children.

Often relational experiences that result in insecure attachment patterns are considered traumatic—thus the term _attachment trauma_. (See chapter 2 for more on trauma in early childhood.) While children's initial attachment experiences can play a huge role in their later relationships, it is important to note that children's social development is complex and that key supportive relationships later on down the road can potentially alter the course of a life on social and neurological levels (Szalavitz and Perry 2010). This is good news for early childhood educators wanting to support children in their healing from early harmful experiences.

Attachment Issues in the Classroom

Virtually all teachers at every level are unaware of the infant and toddler experiences of their students. However, they may see the behavioral clues to insecure attachments or attachment trauma every day, often without realizing what they are seeing. Again, certain children who act out in class may never have developed adequate self-regulation skills. Realizing that children who are hyperactive may not have had the opportunities to develop the neural pathways essential for self-regulation can help adults understand that disciplining these youngsters will require a more complex and compassionate process than traditional models (Bailey 2011). Some other examples of behavior patterns related to insecure attachment issues follow.

Children with attachment trauma may have great difficulty formulating trusting relationships with their teachers and other caring adults. Others may be overly friendly even toward complete strangers (a phenomenon termed "indiscriminate friendliness"). They may defy authority, or they may fear dependency and not ask for assistance. They frequently have little impulse control and have difficulty dealing with new information. When overwhelmed, they sometimes get up and silently walk out of their classroom because they lack the coping skills required to deal effectively with stress (Geddes 2006), such as the threatening prospect of not knowing the answer. They may be extremely sensitive to perceived criticism.

Children (and the teens they will become) with insecure attachment patterns can have social problems that complicate friendships and relationships. They have great difficulty deciphering where their boundaries end and the boundaries of others begin. And they don't know whom to trust (Cozolino 2006). Healthy boundaries permit children and adults to determine how others can treat them, and empower them to say no, when it is essential for their security and health (Szalavitz and Perry 2010). A helpful children's book about boundaries is *Personal Space Camp* by Julia Cook.

Children with attachment trauma are preoccupied with separations and a change in teaching staff. Some children desperately try to be first and in control to avert being left out. Because of experiences of disconnect with care providers and a life of always being on alert, they can present behaviors that are misinterpreted by adults as manipulation. Further complicating the teacher's role, these students interpret standard discipline as yet another rejection (Levine and Kline 2007).

Another difficulty for young students with some form of insecure attachment patterns is understanding sequences of beginning, middle, and ending. Similarly, they may have trouble with understanding the passage of time and continuity, which can affect memory (Perry and Szalavitz 2006). To them, a past incidence of fear or rejection can become an ongoing situation, never ending. This can lead to a sense of hopelessness.

Each of these examples of behavior is just that—an example. No one child will exhibit all of these issues, and just because a child does show a particular tendency or problem does not necessarily mean that he or she has had deeply traumatic attachment experiences. What it *does* mean is that educators who understand the connection between insecure attachments and behavioral missteps should pay attention to behavior that signals possibly deeper problems. Any concerns should increase communication among the educator, the family, and other support staff such as tutors or counselors.

Educators may have great difficultly not feeling anger toward the parents who have not adequately nurtured these children. But research has shown that adults who were unable to form a secure attachment to their parent(s) as infants may not be able to attach to their own infants without sensitive support and coaching (Cozolino 2006). These explanations can help educators move beyond frustration with children's and parents' behavior to address problems at a deeper level.

What Children with Attachment Issues Need from Teachers

There are some specific guidelines teachers can follow to support children with attachment issues, difficult as that may seem in the midst of chaos. Start by posting a full day's schedule in a way all students can understand. This will assure their sense of security and provide a predictable routine, which is especially helpful for young students (Bailey 2011). Offer concrete activities, such as counting, coloring, sorting, and sequencing objects or pictures, as a starting point for deeper learning. Using metaphorical objects to introduce the issue of security and connection, such as boxes, containers, bridges, gates, and castles, can calm anxious children (Geddes 2006). This activity can include drawing, puppet stories, or creative writing for those who can write—see the activities in part 2 of this book for specific ideas.

Geddes (2006) and Bailey (2011) advise teachers to avoid confrontations and not tell insecure children directly what they have to do. Instead, offer suggestions for the entire class. Focus on rules that keep everyone safe, and refer to these rules in every possible situation. Adults interacting with children with insecure attachment styles are advised to respond to the meaning of the child's disconcerting behaviors rather than simply reacting to the outward behaviors. By turning reaction into reflective intervention, adults are likely to be more successful in supporting the child (Geddes 2006). Solid, trusting relationships with adult role models who care for the child every day can help to heal insecure attachment patterns and promote the positive development of skills that children need to succeed (Cozolino 2006).

2. Early Traumatic Stress

Every person experiences a range of stressful events, thoughts, and emotions throughout life. A stress-causing experience can be a difficult job, a dying family member, or the act of crossing a busy street. Each of these events can cause some level of stress that the body and mind will respond to. As discussed in chapter 1, the strength and style of a person's attachment relationships can greatly influence that person's responses to everyday stressors and her willingness to brave, explore, and learn from new or stressful experiences. There is hardly a child alive who has not learned the world can be dangerous and hostile. Here in the United States, words and images of violence pervade children's recreation, entertainment, neighborhoods, and, for some, homes. Ideally, children who experience stressful events will have safe, nurturing relationships with adults who can help them process those stressful events appropriately, but this doesn't always happen. Sometimes a child's experience of a stressful event is far greater than her capability, and the capabilities of available adults, to help process the event.

A first-grade boy was unable to stay in his seat, which was in the row of desks next to the first-floor windows of his classroom. His teacher repeatedly called upon him to return to his seat and was getting frustrated.

He was sent to the school counselor, who was asked to intervene. The counselor knelt down in front of him and gently stroked his hand as they talked. She commented on his pattern of getting out of his seat and asked, "What do you need to have happen so you can stay in your seat?" He responded, "I want to sit in the first row, far away from the windows."

Upon consulting with the boy's mother, the counselor learned that the previous summer, a driver lost control of his car and crashed into their living room window!

Psychologists Peter Levine and Maggie Kline say that trauma "happens when *any* experience stuns us like a bolt out of the blue; it overwhelms us, leaving us altered and disconnected from our bodies. Any coping mechanisms we may have had are undermined, and we feel utterly helpless and hopeless. . . . Trauma is the antithesis of empowerment" (2007, 4). Some common examples of traumatic events are the death of a friend, a physically or emotionally abusive relationship, or a car accident. It is significant, however, that it is not the event itself that traumatizes but a person's experience of that event. If a child feels his life to be in danger, perhaps on a carnival ride or in a swimming pool, such an experience can be traumatizing, regardless of the actual threat present. Traumatic experiences for anyone at any age are fearful and scary. For children, they are especially so because their childlike thinking surmises their life is at risk, even when it is not. Both one-time traumatic events, such as a car accident or loss of a family member, and repeated traumatic events, such as an abusive caregiver, can have a lasting impact on children.

The Body's Stress Reactions

Babette Rothschild says, "Trauma is a psychophysical experience, even when the traumatic event causes no direct bodily harm" (2000, 5). Essentially, in a highly stressful experience, the body begins to prepare either to escape or to fight back. The heart rate increases, pupils dilate, and blood pressure goes up as the body prepares for an emergency. This is often called the "fight-or-flight" response. The body can also have a "freeze" response if it perceives there is not enough time to either flee or fight its way out: the heart rate slows, sensory input decreases, and a person feels disconnected from her body as the body "plays dead" in preparation for injury (Perry 2004).

When the brain and body go into this "emergency mode," other areas of the brain that deal with things like language, logic, and abstract thought are not primarily used. A perceived threat can generate a fight/flight/freeze reaction that is survival driven and automatic (Szalavitz and Perry 2010). It can be said that the brain's emergency response "hijacks" other, possible, slower or more rational responses.

While the body can have a variety of reactions to traumatic events, what is important is that all of these reactions are a physical, neurological response that the body experiences and the brain remembers. The body's response to trauma is a normal reaction to an abnormal experience of insecurity. Levine and Kline say, "Vulnerability to trauma differs from person to person depending on a variety of factors, especially age and trauma history. The younger the child, the more likely she is to be overwhelmed by common occurrences that might not affect an older child or adult" (2007, 4). The stressed child in the following story presented an automatic survival reaction to a perceived threat: the teacher's tone of voice and what he interpreted as angry words. He needed his teacher to use her own powers of self-regulation to help him reclaim his self-control.

A kindergarten class in an urban school had been practicing writing their full names. A very tense and overactive boy had begun to draw and color, when a teacher's aide noticed he had not written his full name on his paper as directed.

She sternly stated that he had not followed directions and needed to write out his full name. The student began to scream, "No," ran around the room, and threw his chair at the aide. This shocked and frightened the entire class.

The aide took him to the office and maintained he had to learn the consequences of his behaviors. None of the children in that class was able to focus on learning for the rest of the afternoon.

Trauma That Lasts: Automatic Survival Reactions to Fears, Threats, and Shame

Humans are born with one hundred billion neural cells. The majority of these cells are not immediately incorporated into synaptic networks—the brain needs to experience life before it will rearrange neural cells into practical networks. Brain development is "use-dependent" (Geddes 2006, 106), which means that a person's experiences help the brain determine which actual neurological connections will be made and which networks will be used again and again. Brain development patterns, then, can be affected by traumatic experiences. In preschoolers for whom a sense of security is not guaranteed, such as a child regularly witnessing domestic or neighborhood violence, more of these neural cells will become integrated into networks that deal with high-stress events. A child's repeated experience of high-stress, traumatic events can begin to build a brain that is acutely sensitive to any potential threat, whether real or perceived (Perry 2004). And because the brain tends to "downshift" out of language- and logic-based areas into an emergency response mode, traumatic experiences and relived memories can cause children to feel totally helpless and powerless, which compounds their sense of shock. Only the thinking brain can devise safety plans or ask for help when seeking safety (Schore 2009). Struggling just to survive can limit children's brain development exclusively to the "flight, fight, or freeze" instinct, greatly reducing their opportunities to solve problems (Cozolino 2006).

Trauma and Children in the Classroom

Children who live with traumatic stress often also have behaviors that disrupt their learning and their classmates' learning (Brendtro, Mitchell, and McCall 2009). Children's experiences of trauma may cause their negative behavior and learning issues, which contribute to teachers' stress and burnout (Levine and Kline 2007). Generally negative behaviors stemming from trauma experiences can be very frustrating for teachers and school personnel. However, these behaviors may come from the brain's overactive stress response and are not always under the "thinking" brain's control (Perry 2004). Volcanic reactions stem from fear: fear of rejection, of being shamed, or of being inadequate. Traumatic stress in children is not a reflection of intellectual capacity, nor is it a mental illness. (However, early traumas that do not receive interventions *can* lead to mental illness in adulthood [Rothschild 2000; Schore 2009].) Children may express their traumatic stress in a variety of ways, but the following are some frequent behaviors.

① Learning Issues

Traumatic stress can be the cause of many learning issues. When students have "downshifted" into an emergency response mode, they may be unable to focus and concentrate as they struggle with intruding worries regarding emotional security. Because they are unable to problem solve and rationalize while their brain is responding to perceived threats, they have serious difficulty deriving meaning and making sense out of what is being taught (Levine and Kline 2007). The automatic stress response also has a profound effect on students' ability to retrieve what was successfully learned, even when not under stress. This can greatly affect test performance—students are not truly able to demonstrate what they have learned or what the teacher has taught.

Students who are unable to apply themselves in school or to other learning activities very often have anxiety and a stress barrier to their "thinking" brain as a result of trauma (Szalavitz and Perry 2010). Teachers cannot teach children operating in their emergency response mode, and these students cannot participate in the learning process.

This is not an excuse for children's behavior or poor achievement, but it offers educators insight and possible explanations for behavior. Teachers who have been informed of the neuroscience of learning and behavioral issues are better able to resist the interpretation of misbehavior as defiant or deficient, allowing them to avoid taking the situations personally (Brendtro, Mitchell, and McCall 2009). The good news is that traumatized students may be hypervigilant to threat, but they are not always operating out of a paralyzed emergency response. They may have good moments, and great teachers can learn to channel those good moments into a great learning experience.

② Understanding Cause and Effect

Children who live with certain kinds of traumatic stress also have great difficulty understanding cause and effect. Depending on the levels of chaos and discipline in their environment, they may be unable to determine a logical or direct correlation between their behavior and the disciplinary action taken by family members or staff. Unfortunately, sometimes poor discipline is determined more by the state of mind of the disciplining adult than by the child's action or the "cause" itself, and is naturally illogical to the child (Szalavitz and Perry 2010). If the adult's reactions are not consistent, then a child has few opportunities to identify the connections between events and consequences.

Educators generally assume all children understand cause and effect. But if understanding was never established, the student may have great difficulty learning science and math skills. Traumatic stress affects students' sense of time and can interfere with their ability to understand sequencing and the meaning of numbers. Students who live with traumatic stress may require repeated opportunities to internalize and trust what their teacher is inferring and what the classroom rules represent or mean so they can begin to trust their teacher and the consistency of their environment.

③ Physical Reactions

Children who have experienced trauma often have heightened startle responses and fear of situations that remind them of previous scary events. They may have intrusive and repeated thoughts and images (Perry 2004). They often struggle with self-regulation and empathy and are moody. They may be highly sensitive to issues of fairness and easily upset by separations and changes in routines. Traumatic stress can also cause children to complain about nightmares and to have trouble sleeping. Sensitive teachers can learn to trust their instincts for the appropriateness of a child's developmental processes and behaviors. While each of these behaviors alone does not necessarily mean that a child is suffering from traumatic stress, the trauma-informed educator will be aware of behaviors that should prompt further investigation into the reason for those behaviors. In the story that follows, hearing the sounds again of a fearful experience was a powerful trigger for a traumatic stress reaction that at first glance appeared to be misbehavior. The sounds of a previous frightening event can place a child back in that moment, and the fear is relived.

A kindergarten student in an urban school was comfortably following directions on a numbers lesson when a fire truck and police cars with sirens blaring drove past his first-floor classroom window. The child jumped up, put his hands over his ears, and ran screaming from his room into the hall. His teacher later learned his family home had burned during the past summer.

Seeming Inability to Hear Words

Perhaps one of the most frustrating experiences for teachers is when a student defies the rules. Often teachers interpret a student's inability to hear and understand consequences as defiance, which adds to a teacher's frustrations (Perry 2004). For instance, a second-grade teacher is moving her class into the hall on their way to lunch. The teacher sternly reminds the class of the hallway rules: no pushing or running. Within one minute, the second boy in line pushes the boy ahead of him aside and runs toward the cafeteria. After the teacher catches up to him, she protests, "What were you thinking? You know the rules!"

Although this may seem logical, another possible explanation is that the student didn't hear his teacher's words or the rules because they were accompanied by a stern facial expression and a harsh voice. He responded with a survival reaction activated by the tone of voice and facial expression. Upon hearing and seeing what he interpreted to be a threat, the student's oversensitive brain quickly shifted into preparation for a perceived threat. If the child heard any words in his emergency state, he heard "pushing and running," and that's what he did. But the boy could not express his fear in words, and when he was unable to offer any explanation for his actions, his teacher very naturally considered him defiant. This is not an excuse for the unacceptable behavior but is a possible explanation for the evidence presented (Perry 2004; Schore 2009). Remember that the child isn't the problem.

A third grader in an urban elementary school was unanimously labeled the worst child in the building. During lunch, the entire multipurpose room was in turmoil due to his total lack of self-regulation.

The all-day kindergarten teacher's room was next to the multipurpose room, and her class took their trays to their classroom to eat in order to avoid the chaos. The principal asked the teacher if this boy could also eat his lunch in her room to reduce the chaos in the cafeteria.

What could she say? The next day at noon, when she heard a knock at her door, she picked up a clipboard, opened the door, and said with a smile, "Welcome! I have been asking for an assistant teacher since September, and here you are!"

The clipboard had two tasks on it: reading to the children every day and teaching the nine children who had not mastered the task of tying their shoelaces. He read to the kindergarten class each lunch period, which they loved.

The teacher reported with surprise and pride that when this boy walked down the hall, the other students there would walk as close to the walls as possible to avoid connecting with him, while her kindergartners would run up to him with hugs. The boy's behavioral change was not exhibited in any other place within or outside the building, as he felt secure only in the kindergarten classroom with the teacher he trusted.

What Children with Unprocessed Trauma Need from Their Teachers

Trauma-informed teachers and schools recognize that all children need emotional and physical security in order to learn, and this security is absolutely critical for students who are experiencing traumatic stress. Children who have experienced trauma need time to trust that they will always be respected and never shamed or rejected. Ideally, this means that students should not experience threats when an educator or other school staff person is with them—in their classrooms, in the cafeteria, on the playground, or on the bus. Solid, trusting relationships between all students and staff increase learning and reduce behavioral issues. Relationships are more essential for students than any other part of education—more than laptops or other electronic hardware, which are often seen as important by the community (Cozolino 2013).

Moreover, trauma-informed educators understand that many troubling behaviors are caused by fear and stress. They are clear in their understanding that troubling behaviors are *stress* behaviors, not intentional misbehaviors (Brendtro, Mitchell, and McCall 2009; Levine and Kline 2007; Perry 2004). This is a critical aspect of trauma-informed education.

An urban kindergarten class had several children with severe behavior issues stemming from a lack of attachment *and* profound insecurity or trauma—these children repeatedly talked about suicide. The explosive actions and screams of these students shocked and scared the entire class, and learning shut down. Some classmates voiced their discomfort, and the teacher called a class meeting about the issue.

The teacher explained that every child should have the opportunity to feel totally safe and valued and that unexpected actions by others or sudden changes in the schedule can cause these children to feel very threatened and scared. He led his class using strict ground rules to determine what the class might do to help their classmates deal with their deep fears. They discussed how to help these students feel safe and a part of the classroom family again.

The suggestions were printed on a poster and hung in the front of the room. The boys with the grave behavior issues were included in the discussions. The explosive episodes slowly began to subside, and the class worked together as more of a unit.

Trauma-informed teachers also realize that stressed students intensely watch teachers' body language and nonverbal behaviors more than they listen to the teachers' words (Perry 2004). For example, they learn that one easy way to assure and calm a student is to offer a smile. Tense students benefit greatly when their teachers use the sensory, body-focused language of the survival brain. Teachers can help calm tense students by referring to the physical sensations of being upset and reassuring them that these sensations are normal: the bodily feeling of "butterflies in the tummy," "a lump in the throat," tense muscles, tingling, jumpiness, dizziness, numbness, or a tightening in the chest (Levine and Kline 2007). Sensations are *experienced*, so using descriptive terms resonates with children. Mindfulness, or the ability to sense what children are experiencing and be attuned and responsive to their feelings and interactions (Ogden 2009), becomes a teacher's true gift to overwhelmed children; it means children are "feeling felt" (Levine and Kline 2007, 302).

Children with traumatic stress sometimes get stuck in a frozen memory of fear. Describing possible sensations will connect with tense children and possibly help them process such a troubling or unconscious memory, bringing relief to the children. Such relief can restore access to the learning process. Traumatic memories and the stress that envelopes them are recorded through the senses of sound, sight, touch, and aroma. Such memories can be reactivated through the senses and not by words alone (Rothschild 2000). Teaching children about deep breathing and how it can bring them a calm sense of relief can also help (Levine and Kline 2007).

Instead of asking "why" questions, ask, "Where in your body do you sense being upset?" Or if children are not able to articulate an answer, ask them to show what the ache feels like. Invite children to draw how they are feeling with colored scribbles, lines, and shapes (Steele and Malchiodi 2012). Another option is to invite children to sit in a chair and push their feet onto the floor as hard as they can. Ask them, "Do you notice a sense of increased strength within you when you push your feet onto the floor?" When children have calmed, say, "Now you are safe, and I am here to keep you safe." Understanding sensations permits children to be more intuitive and confident.

Traumatized students can be calmed and open to deep learning when they sense their teacher is attuned to their inner thoughts and emotions (Bailey 2011). This enables the students to feel understood and results in a sense of security and trust.

In early childhood education classrooms, tense and agitated children can be calmed by working with flubber—a cool, soft substance that is delightful and calming to touch. It can be offered as an incentive to help strengthen a child's self-regulation skills (see the activity section in chapter 7 for a recipe for flubber). The longer a child stays self-regulated, the stronger the coping skills for managing unexpected changes in routine (Bailey 2011).

Differentiating between Traumatic Stress Behaviors and ADHD

Early child education classes are the critical times for recognizing and responding to persistent and troubling patterns of behaviors in children. Early child education sets the foundation for a child's future self-understanding of school and being a student. Thus, it is imperative that classrooms and teachers provide resolutions to behavioral issues as opposed to engaging in labeling a child.

Trauma-informed educators recognize that traumatic stress and attention-deficit/hyperactivity disorder (ADHD) present very similar behavior patterns of acting out and disturbing the class (Perry 2004). Since there is no specific medical test for determining traumatic stress or ADHD, ADHD can easily be misdiagnosed when students actually are exhibiting symptoms of traumatic stress (Steele and Malchiodi 2012). While educators should not play the role of a diagnosing expert, they can contribute to the evidence-gathering process as caring adults trying to get children the help they need. Trauma-informed teachers recognize that hyperactivity following a single acute stress is a normal reaction that does not mean the child has ADHD. In addition, the current diagnosis for ADHD is not effective for children living with chronic stress, according to the National Institute for Trauma and Loss in Children (Steele and Malchiodi 2012).

Prescribing medications may be simpler and easier than implementing measures that provide emotional security, but medications do not always heal or strengthen the neural connections in the brain; sometimes they only manage the symptoms. Misdiagnoses allow the real cause to go undetected and without any intervention (Steele and Malchiodi 2012). Trauma-informed educators can help children by supporting a careful and honest diagnosis process that will give students the help they need.

Stressed and hyperactive children benefit from <u>teachers who capitalize on students' strengths</u>, including ones traditionally not part of academic learning, such as <u>art, music, creative writing, or interpretive dance</u>. Introducing subjects and activities of personal interest to children will help them strengthen their self-regulation and ability to focus.

Trauma-informed teachers present concepts and new knowledge in small portions, reinforced by hands-on activities. Stressed children require opportunities to integrate new information into their real-life experiences and understandings. One way to do this is to encourage children to relate new information to their life experiences through stories or drawings. Another way to strengthen stressed children's sense of security is to connect them with students from several grades above them as buddies or companions.

I have had the privilege of working with early child educators who were so dedicated and caring that they collected clothes for students who needed replacements. Trauma-informed teachers are equally attentive to the internal sense of stability and confidence of stressed children. Teachers today have a noble opportunity to make a lifelong difference in the lives of fragile young children.

3. Implementing the Trauma-Informed Classroom

Fifteen years ago, schools would tell me in all seriousness that they had no traumatized students. Although it is widely known that military veterans frequently suffer from post-traumatic stress disorder (PTSD), many educators and other adults are unaware of a similar form of traumatic stress in children. Maybe because we all sincerely want childhood to be secure and joyful, we find it difficult to acknowledge that little children can be traumatized. No school would fail to provide essential emergency medical care for a child hurt on the playground, but acknowledging wounds that are invisible is still challenging for many adults. Adults often say, "Oh, he'll outgrow these behaviors," or "It's just a phase." Regrettably, children who have been traumatized are often misidentified as strong willed and defiant! Trauma-informed educators fully realize that children who are unable to exercise self-regulation are fearful, not simply disobedient (Bailey 2011).

Today educators and schools are beginning to acknowledge that attachment or event-based trauma is a barrier to learning. Even *Education Week*, a leading education tabloid, has begun to address the link between trauma and children's poor academic achievement (Sparks 2012). Adopting a trauma-informed, alternative disciplinary protocol represents a great paradigm shift in education for distressed students as well as their classmates and teachers. As described in chapters 1 and 2, educators can gain insight into behavioral problems by understanding the neural science behind many issues of concern to teachers. These insights afford teachers a greater capacity for attunement and empathy. Students who are propelled into the spotlight by their disturbing behaviors tend to be the most fragile children in their schools. For behavioral interventions to be effective, educators must acknowledge that the root causes of problematic behaviors can stem from insecure attachments or traumatic experiences. This chapter will discuss some ways educators can become more sensitive to children's traumatic experiences in understanding and addressing behavioral issues.

An Example of Trauma–Informed Teaching

I recently participated in an educational research project at an elementary school titled "Growing the Brain." This trauma-informed brief project was based on the notion that an emotionally secure environment with positive relationships between students and teachers can rewire and reorganize the brains of stressed children. Our hope was that we could reduce the emotional, cognitive, and behavioral difficulties of the stressed students. Our intentions were to keep students within their positive range of self-regulation throughout the school day.

The goal of this project was to enhance the academic achievement of all students in the participating classrooms. The staff involved were teachers from one kindergarten, one first-grade, and one second-grade classroom, plus behavioral coaches and Title I teachers. They were asked to integrate a sensory healing activity from the first edition of *Making It Better* and other resources into core curriculum assignments once a week. They were each provided with a copy of the book and received twenty hours of training.

An activity that became a focus of the K–2 classrooms was the compelling eye and hand rituals from Becky Bailey's book *I Love You Rituals*. Maintaining deep eye contact while gently touching the hands of a child can stimulate growth and strengthening of the prefrontal cortex, especially of children that did not have the opportunity to form a solid attachment in infancy. The prefrontal cortex is the area of the brain that is involved in self-regulation, stress management, and empathy (see chapter 1).

Touch and warm, friendly eye contact can provide nurturing that was possibly missed during infancy. Young students were absolutely thrilled with the loving interaction and could not get enough of it. Students were encouraged to engage in the rituals with younger siblings, relatives, and neighborhood youngsters. Including older students in the loving rituals with younger students doubles the positive results. Here are a couple examples of these rituals:

A Wonderful Woman Who Lived in a Shoe
A wonderful woman lived in a shoe.
She had so many children
she knew exactly what to do.
She held them,
she rocked them,
and tucked them in bed.
"I love you, I love you,"
is what she said.
(Bailey 2000, 59)

Instructions: Say the first line and take one of the child's hands and give it a gentle rub. Touch each finger of that hand as you mention all the children she had.

As you say, "She held them," fold the fingers of the child's hand into a ball and wrap both your hands around the child's, swaying from side to side as though you were rocking the hand as you finish the ritual.

Twinkle, Twinkle Little Star
Twinkle, twinkle little star,
What a wonderful child you are!
With bright eyes and nice
    round cheeks,
Talented person from head to feet.
Twinkle, twinkle little star,
What a wonderful child you are!
(Bailey 2000, 63)

Instructions: Ask the children to raise their hands with you and touch their fingertips on each other's hands as you repeat the verse. End by holding the hands of the children in yours as you gaze into their eyes.

Managing the Trauma-Informed Environment

There are several things teachers can do to implement a trauma-informed environment. In addition to educating themselves on behaviors and concerns of traumatized children, they can create a safe, supportive environment for all children, which includes sensitivity to highly vigilant children who may need more space and attention to their needs. Trauma-informed teachers should be aware that they are not expected to "cure" children or diagnose children independently—if there is any concern that a child has experienced trauma, caregivers, counselors, and other support staff should immediately be involved. Then the trauma-informed teacher can support the student along with the rest of the class through trauma-informed practices such as the ones below. See the section on counselors' roles in chapter 4 for more on involving support staff.

Strengthening Self-Regulation

Self-regulation is now considered a stronger predictor of achievement than IQ, according to Duckworth and Seligman (2005). Neuroscience offers an explanation for why young children with insecure attachments or deep losses of security often have a lack of self-regulation or self-control: they haven't strengthened the neural pathways required to master these skills (Cozolino 2006).

A five-year-old boy who had continuous problems being a playmate picked up a handful of playground mulch and threw it at a classmate. The targeted classmate did not rebuke the boy and instead said, "Why don't we shake hands and become friends?" The troubled boy, totally surprised by the unexpected congeniality, gingerly offered his hand. They became playmates, much to the teacher's surprise.

A student with strong self-regulation skills can also inspire a youngster with poor social patterns to grow and strengthen his self-regulation skills. Children can benefit from classmates and teachers who model solid self-regulation skills.

Teachers can help students practice self-control by practicing it themselves. Current research indicates students with minimal self-regulation can strengthen their skills when influenced by a teacher who consistently practices self-control. Students who trust their teacher's ability to maintain self-regulation can better maintain continuous self-control themselves (Bailey 2011). This does not mesh with the old idea teachers may have heard in preservice trainings that outward clues of strength—such as being stern and formal the first six weeks—are what teachers should strive for. Today educators have a choice: Is the goal to build self-regulation skills in students or to focus on children who are subdued because of fear? Students who sense emotional security will achieve greater heights. Since test scores are becoming a significant portion of teacher evaluation, maintaining emotional security has taken on more significance.

Here are some suggestions for strengthening self-regulation: When students are not able to function at a high level and their brains are operating on high-alert mode, they may present physical actions of aggression or engage in blistering verbal outbursts. Or they may not be able to hear their teacher when functioning at this level (Perry 2004). Teachers who understand this know to comment on what they are seeing instead of a student's words. For example, the teacher says, "I see you looking at the ceiling," instead of "Don't use that language here." Such statements of observations—I see you are looking at the ceiling—are best made in a nonjudgmental and relaxed manner. When said in this manner, the child's shoulders are likely to drop as she takes a deep breath and relaxes. She may not have actually heard the teacher's words, but she has been assured by the teacher's own self-regulation and calmness (Bailey 2011). Seeing this calmness take over, the teacher says, "I'm guessing something has upset you. What do you need to have happen so you can feel safer? In my room everyone has a right to feel safe!" This exchange will convince the student that the teacher is primarily interested in building a resolution, not disciplining the child. Discipline rarely builds resolutions or strengthens self-regulation skills. The more a child is able to stay self-regulated, the greater will be his ability to remain calm and learn. The best discipline is respect and caring (Grille 2005). Responding with a calm reaction can help return trust and calmness and reinstate the learning process (Levine and Kline 2007). The more time distressed children remain calm, function at a high cognitive level, and practice self-regulation, the quicker they will strengthen their self-control skills and engage in deep learning (Brendtro, Mitchell, and McCall 2009).

Emotional Security

Emotional security is an essential, primary factor in implementing a trauma-informed educational system. It guarantees all students freedom from real or perceived fears of being rejected or shamed. For this to occur, the discipline policy must be based on holding students accountable for building resolutions (see chapter 4's section on restorative discipline for more). And, of course, a policy in name only is not enough. The principal must lead the staff, and everyone must be in agreement to practice this approach for it to work. Emotional security is built on the concept of mutual respect and role-modeled by all adults and expected of all students. Trusting relationships between all adults and students are the foundation of an emotionally secure environment for deep learning and achievement. Becoming a trauma-informed school requires commitment and patience from all involved.

Offering Healing Opportunities

Students who are living with unprocessed traumatic stress often feel trapped in their memories and an overwhelming sense of loss. Steele and Malchiodi (2012) say the only way traumatized students can access frozen scary memories is through sensory movement of some kind. Certainly the body retains traumatic memories as much as the brain does, which is why sensory healing is essential to the overall healing process. Movement of the hands in play, art, and writing fulfills this requirement, and all these activities can fit into classrooms. Moving in rhythm, such as dance, song, or rap, also permits this access (Steele and Malchiodi 2012).

When children realize that accessing a scary memory will not overwhelm them, because they are in an emotionally safe environment, they can begin to process the hurt. An emotionally safe environment assures children that support from a trusted adult is available. This process permits children to slowly gain the confidence essential for addressing the frozen fear and employs the problem-solving capacity of the thinking brain. Children begin to realize they can put the gripping fear to rest. This permits them to conclude that the negative experience should never have happened (Kagan 2004). Through the healing process, students can move on to face the future in spite of the experience. They are empowered to proceed with their development, become an active learner, and pursue their destiny (Brendtro, Mitchell, and McCall 2009).

The key is to remember that it is difficult for words to reach the brain of an actively distressed student. Educators cannot "talk" children out of the irritating and frustrating behaviors that are a result of traumatic stress. Many educators are taught to say, "Use your words" when children are physically acting out a hurt or frustration. Trauma-informed teachers understand saying this may add to the disconnect and stress between teacher and student, who may not be functioning on a words-and-logic level. Trauma-informed educators realize that telling a student to calm down and make better choices also does not work, because a traumatized student may not be able to process logical choices (Levine and Kline 2007).

Likewise, traditional discipline cannot be used to address and heal the cause of these behaviors. Children experience healing when they are able to externalize the memories that would otherwise eventually disempower them (Steele and Malchiodi 2012).

Identifying and Labeling Feelings and Sensations

Being able to identify and label feelings and sensations is a preventive tool as well as a vital step in the healing process. Many young children are bewildered by feelings, which are intangible and difficult to explain to a child. Some may have been told not to have some of them, like anger and jealousy. Feelings are abstract and uncertain issues for children. Frequently children try to ignore uncomfortable feelings rather than using the energy of their feelings to help them make sense of life and keep them safe (Kagan 2004; Perry and Szalavitz 2006).

Children need safe places to practice naming and identifying their own feelings and those of others. Identifying the feelings in photographs showing facial expressions is a great way to practice; so is looking in a mirror and making faces showing sad, scared, excited, happy, and so on. The more comfortable children are in identifying and labeling feelings, the more able they will be to comfortably own them and be empowered by them. The goal is to encourage students to move beyond the customary glad, sad, and bad. The greater the comfort in naming feelings, the deeper will be the realization that they are natural and normal.

Because feelings are so abstract and confusing to youngsters, especially to distressed ones, adults are recommended not to immediately use abstract feeling words to address hypersensitive or traumatized children. Instead, adults should use the words that describe body sensations or sensory experiences that all young students have experienced. Some examples are *twitchy, butterflies, jittery, shaky, squishy, tingly, tight, frozen, dizzy, calm, relaxed, smooth, loose, spacey,* and *empty.* These expressions immediately resonate with young students, especially anxious ones. Some of the healing activities in this book are directed at naming feelings. For further information, Peter A. Levine and Maggie Kline offer extensive insights into the language of sensations in their book *Trauma through a Child's Eyes.*

4. Trauma-Informed Discipline

The trauma-informed education movement aims to help children and their families become resilient to the stresses and adversity they may encounter in life (Grille 2005). When children and their families are resilient, they have the support and strength to handle difficulties they experience, large or small. Traumatic stress no longer has to be a child's destiny. Trauma-informed education has the opportunity to reshape society and build a world in which children can thrive. Trauma-informed early childhood educators have the profound opportunity to restore dignity, self-respect, and hope to distressed students.

A trauma-informed educational atmosphere will include discipline policies that are influenced by an understanding of brain development and behavior related to trauma. Children who act out, seek attention, or behave in sometimes frightening ways are often in need of discipline that can address needs far beyond their behaviors. This is what trauma-informed discipline is all about.

The greatest gift adults can give to students who have not received nonjudgmental support is to believe in their capabilities. This gift goes far beyond the transference of academic knowledge. Trusting relationships can create an internal biological environment that supports positive learning and growth. Positive adult role models truly offer insecure students the gift of life: resilience (Brendtro, Mitchell, and McCall 2009). Supporting relationships can stimulate positive emotions, neuroplasticity, and learning; compassion, love, and warmth have the power to heal the brain (Cozolino 2006).

Bullying Behaviors

Caring teachers can be stunned by the lack of empathy expressed by some of today's children. However, informed teachers recognize such behaviors are often a sign of deeper and more significant internal problems. Children cannot acquire empathy from someone who doesn't have it. Disciplinary actions do not generate empathy, and certain discipline methods may hinder its development. Current research affirms that empathy must be experienced and received from someone of significance to the young child (Szalavitz and Perry 2010). Adults do not "teach" empathy, they give it through mindfulness and being attuned. Trauma-informed educators appreciate the value of empathy to society and students. For more on traumatic stress and suggestions for responding to related behaviors, see chapter 2.

Students who engage in bullying behaviors tend to be children who have witnessed family aggression or have received harsh discipline (Kagan 2004). Generally, they are youngsters who feel powerless and hopeless about issues in their lives (Szalavitz and Perry 2010). Richard Kagan suggests that children who live with violence learn that violence works for the aggressor—the aggressor's goal is accomplished—and these children are more likely to try similar tactics with other people or animals as a way to deal with being powerless. Kagan suggests that when these children see fear in the eyes of their target, they experience relief from their own internalized sense of helplessness, and this sense of power they experience overcomes any apprehensions they may have regarding possible disciplinary actions. Many schools have learned that threatening discipline does not stop bullying behaviors, although it may change where they take place, namely, away from school (Kagan 2004). Simply moving the location of the bullying impacts victims, who have been assured that adults at school will make things right and end the bullying. Implying that adults can control bullying behaviors fools no one.

Preventing Bullying

Trauma-informed schools implement proactive responses to the issue of bullying; they reframe the issue to support student-centered responses that focus on every student feeling safe as opposed to rules that have been broken. Trauma-informed teachers take note of aggressive, uncaring behaviors from day one and respond with calm stability that focuses on safety. Threats are not used, nor is shame or rejections.

Students who engage in bullying tend to be very savvy youngsters and quickly sense when adults practice mutual respect or not. They are never fooled by power plays, which greatly undermine trust and the sense of security. Adults who focus on winning in their interactions with children communicate to children that the needs of the child are not important or valid. Children who are not respected can develop an attitude of getting even (Szalavitz and Perry 2010). Students who have lost a sense of security have an overwhelming need to "save face" and are extremely sensitive to rejections, but they do respond well when they sense they are valued. Trauma-informed schools and teachers find ways to reach these students and utilize their deep need in generating an environment of fairness and trust. Often these students have great leadership qualities that can be developed and utilized (Kagan 2004).

The challenge for adults is how to guide those who bully so they can experience relief from their helplessness in ways that do not create new victims. Strategies that may have worked with aggressive students in the past may not work with today's youngsters, especially those whose early childhood insecurities have created a new childhood model for everyone (Cozolino 2013). Trauma-informed education offers a reliable way to prevent bullying behaviors because it focuses on the emotional needs of children.

The key factor is not to ignore the very first indicators of distressed and powerless children. Teasing, taunting, and name-calling along with rejecting and exclusion behaviors are *not* simply kids being kids and cannot be ignored. Building connectedness within the classroom and school will help. One suggestion is to have a "Mix It Up at Lunch" day, when students sit at new tables with classmates they may not know well (read more at www.tolerance.org/mix-it-up). True preventive strategies rely on caring adults to guarantee insecure children that they are safe, and these strategies must be in place on the first day of school. After that, the primary strategy is to manage behaviors before they become patterns of aggression. This is prevention at its best. Educators must remember that children with traumatic stress have to transform those memories before they can effectively practice conflict management. Distressed and anxious students often engage in "antisocial" behaviors because they have experienced the use of power by someone else and are trying to feel that they are powerful and safe and that they will survive (Perry 2004). Educators need to direct distressed students toward ways to feel in charge of their lives that do not create new victims. The activities in part 2 include such healing opportunities.

Above all, remember that trauma-informed educators and other adults have the unique opportunity to address the needs of children who fear rejection and exclusion. This approach has the best chance of averting bullying behavior patterns before they become a set routine.

End Time-Outs, Detentions, and Suspensions

The use of time-outs for young children has been questioned in the past decade. The assumption that the isolated child is constructively reflecting on her wrongdoing has been difficult to prove and is doubtful, especially for children with security issues. Time-outs present an experience of rejection and shame for stressed children. Time-outs do not necessarily rewire the brain or heal the brain of deep fears, insecurities, or shame (Szalavitz and Perry 2010). Consequences and punishments used as discipline can be counterproductive. Stressed students have difficulty understanding the correlation between the offense and the punishment, and their confusion exacerbates their issues of self-regulation. All educators have to seriously consider the safety of all students in their classroom. The challenge is to guarantee safety without undermining achievement (Szalavitz and Perry 2010).

Detentions and suspensions, which are consequence discipline, assume that students understand their own behaviors and automatically sense how to rectify the situation, and do not provide the child with constructive alternatives or solutions. How can schools fulfill their mandate to educate students who are suspended? Many schools have adopted a zero tolerance approach to bullying and violence, which has led to more children being suspended. In a report from the American Psychological Association's Zero Tolerance Task Force, researchers present a strong critique of zero tolerance policies. The report states that zero tolerance policies rarely act as a deterrent to students who have been disciplined under them, and the policies disproportionately affect students of color (2008).

And then there are schools with teachers and staff who stop and ask with genuine care, "You're upset today. What's wrong?" Trauma-informed education does not expect discipline that deepens fears and shame to turn around a troubled and troubling student. Rather, it provides insights into possible causes of behavior issues and what the student requires to feel safe and secure.

Restorative Discipline

What's a teacher to do with children who cannot accept disciplinary actions or follow rules? Aren't teachers responsible for the safety of all the children in their classrooms? Trauma-informed schools recognize that no one is safe within a school unless everyone senses safety and security. It takes only one distressed student to cause harm to many others.

Restorative discipline is an approach that offers a proactive way to maintain classroom predictability and safety as well as help children with attachment issues to strengthen their self-regulation and meet classroom expectations (Bailey 2011). Restorative discipline holds that relationships are the foundation of secure learning environments and that every student and staff person is a valued member of the school. Mutual respect is practiced throughout the building and playground. The approach addresses the root causes of the discipline problems rather than the symptoms.

Restorative discipline focuses on the harm done by the incident, not the rules broken. It works toward a solution that meets the emotional and security needs of *all* parties harmed by the unacceptable actions and gives them a voice through collaborative problem solving by all involved. The rule is never more important than the student. With this approach, the unmet needs of the student who caused the harm are also addressed. The violator is asked what a fair process or resolution might look like. And the student is held accountable for building a solution that restores a sense of comfort and security to the classroom community. Rejection and shaming are not acceptable (Amstutz and Mullet 2005).

Resources for the Trauma-Informed School

Counselors' Special Role in a Trauma-Informed School

Counselors in the early elementary grades have a unique opportunity to be a change agent in the lives of traumatized children. Counselors often meet with the children who have difficulty meeting the expectations of adults within school and at home. These children desperately need an anchor they can trust and share their concerns with. Distressed children often feel invisible, and sensitive counselors can break through such barriers.

Counselors may have the greatest opportunity to reach through distressed children's silent fears and strengthen their belief in themselves. Counselors in elementary schools can have a lifelong effect on children with stress because their young brains are malleable and they are at the beginning of their roles as learners. Counselors can help stressed students realize that they are not alone with their fears and that their startling body reactions are normal, considering the experiences they have had (Steele and Malchiodi 2012).

Elementary counselors can support classroom teachers in understanding that the frustrating behaviors they frequently see or hear are actually an adaptive coping strategy by a distressed child. Counselors can guide staff in refraining from pathologizing these behaviors.

Creating a Safe Place

A purposeful way to assure children with traumatic stress and minimal self-regulation skills that they are secure is to offer a safe retreat area in the classroom. The more they can stay in a state of self-control, the more they will successfully cope with unexpected changes, stay calm, and avoid meltdowns. This is important for academic achievement and in the creation and maintenance of predictable school and classroom climates (Levine and Kline 2007).

Within a classroom, Becky A. Bailey suggests placing a beanbag chair in a partially secluded part of the room under a sign that reads "Safe Place." Directions from teachers explain how children can calm themselves and strengthen their self-regulation. Beanbag chairs are advised because they make contact with large portions of the body, thereby creating a sense of snug security (2011). The purpose of the Safe Place is to encourage a child who is losing self-control and getting upset to choose to visit the beanbag chair as a personal way to strengthen self-regulation. Placement in the Safe Place is not imposed but is intended to strengthen an early elementary child's ability to self-calm. Another suggestion from Bailey is to provide access to symbolic ways to relax, including hugging a small plush toy, squeezing a ball, and cuddling with a little soft blanket. Children can be reminded to smile and take a deep breath, which increases the oxygen flow to the brain. Early elementary children can be encouraged to write or draw how they are calming themselves.

Students who have recently experienced a major crisis, such as a house fire, a break-in at home, or being homeless, may need a longer, complete sanctuary when recent traumatic memories overwhelm them. Outfitting an available empty room in the school as a Safe Room can provide this sanctuary and help the distressed child and the classroom sustain a calm climate (Lovre 2006). The student who needs to visit the Safe Room will have to be accompanied at all times, maybe by a parent helper.

I have found a Safe Room works best when equipped with several large balls for bouncing, a walking beam, and a rocking horse for stress relief. Crayons and paper are also essential. For respite rooms to provide assured sanctuary, they must never be used to harbor students who have engaged in injurious behavior to classmates and are out of self-control. Safe Rooms or respite rooms are an integral component of a trauma-informed school. Trainings for Safe Room staff or parent volunteers is absolutely essential (Lovre 2006). It is imperative that the adults who support children in Safe Rooms are able to demonstrate constant self-regulation.

In-Service Training for All Staff

Providing training in conflict management for the staff and students is a purposeful effort for the total student body. Conflict resolution is best taught by everyday examples. Students watch the way adults around them resolve issues and use power. Children practice what they see adults do more than what they hear adults say (Brendtro, Mitchell, and McCall 2009).

The process of becoming a trauma-informed school requires all staff to receive in-depth training about topics that include brain development, attachment issues, and traumatic stress. Office and cafeteria personnel, playground monitors, tutors, bus drivers, and any other staff who interact with children and contribute to the overall school climate need to be included in the training.

As new staff enter the school, they will need to be trained too. As essential as in-service training is, it will be most effective when attendance is voluntary, except for new staff who are joining the school family and are free to embrace what is expected. Training can be a condition of employment, since the process requires great patience and personal ownership. Staff members who find trauma-informed education works for them should be invited to share their experience, as they can be very influential advocates.

School nurses can provide support to classroom teachers when they have been trauma informed. Stressed children very naturally express physical health complaints that do not always fit a straightforward medical diagnosis. School nurses (and other adults) can provide stable and comforting relief for children with traumatic stress simply by listening without judging.

Reaching Out to Families

Adults generally raise their children similar to the way they were raised as children. All families everywhere want their children to be well mannered and responsible and to have a conscience. Societies differ greatly in how to parent children to achieve this and on how to shape children's understandings of power and aggression. In some societies, nurturing children is considered unmanly, while in others, strength and courage are integrated into protecting and respecting children. Consequence-based parenting is not uncommon in Western society, but is far from meeting the needs of children with traumatic stress or the goals of trauma-informed care (Forbes and Post 2006). Consequences do not help children learn problem solving. They impose shame and helplessness instead (Szalavitz and Perry 2010; Grille 2005).

Engaging the families of stressed and anxious students is very difficult. Connecting with parents can be made easier by identifying the goal of the outreach as a way to assure the safety of their children. Educators should not use initial communications with families to address trauma-informed parenting. This may result in some parents assuming the school is identifying them as the cause of their children's anxiety. An approach that may connect with families is referred to as love-based parenting (Forbes and Post 2006). It offers an alternative to consequence-based parenting.

Love-based parenting affirms that addressing the behaviors of a child is not an evaluation of the parent's effectiveness. Love-based parenting focuses on the importance of relationships and emphasizes that a conscience is developed through loving relationships, not consequences. It can reinforce a trauma-informed education and support the goal of generating cooperative and respectful student behaviors. Consider collaborating with area social service agencies or the faith community within the school district for such an outreach.

All caring adults sincerely want children to be responsible, to fit into society, and to be respectful of adults. However, as adults teach children to do these things, they must take into account the stressful situations some children may find themselves in. Successful educators understand and help students develop skills that will be useful throughout life in all of society.

5. The Unique Grieving Process for Each Child

All children experience losses as a part of growing up. As with trauma, the nature of the loss itself is secondary to *how* a loss is processed. Unprocessed losses are cumulative for children. Each new loss or separation can cause emotional pressure and reopen old wounds, contributing to a child's difficulty believing in a positive future (Szalavitz and Perry 2010). Many losses can cause a dramatic change in a child's daily life—anything from the loss of a pet or a best friend moving away to the death of a parent, grandparent, or care provider. The effect of the loss is compounded when it is coupled with another personal, family, or community challenge. An unexpected loss or separation, such as a move to low-income housing after a divorce, a sibling's death from cancer, or brutal violence toward family members, can overwhelm the coping skills of a child. And losses for children with traumatic stress are doubly severe because of the grave sense of doom or insecurity that may already be a part of their lives.

Sometimes the support systems and coping skills of the family or other adults in the child's life are inadequate to assist the child through the grief process. Schools often represent a safe place for students to process their grief and experience organized and predictable structure. School can provide opportunities for relationships with nurturing role models and consistent routines along with clear limits. If there is concern that a child is deeply depressed, refer the child for evaluation and counseling. See appendix A of this book for guidelines.

Grieving Children

The grieving process often involves recalling images and memories of the deceased or inaccessible person, animal, place, or object. Grieving students may dwell on things they used to do with the deceased while they reject old friends and classmates and sit alone. Or they can become the "class clown," disrupt the class, and instigate fights. Sometimes grieving students will seem unmoved by the loss yet become very sensitive and tearful, often unprovoked.

Grieving students often seem to be regressing or going back to behaviors they had practiced earlier. Children also have creative ways of integrating their understandings into adult perspectives that need to be respected (as an example, see the story that follows). Children experiencing stress will automatically return to standard behaviors that helped them feel safe and secure when they were younger, such as thumb sucking, hair twisting, or rocking (Levine and Kline 2007). These are natural survival behaviors and are part of the child's coping and processing strategy. Each person's grieving process is integral to his healing and is an essential component of recovery.

A neighbor family was arranging the funeral of a grandparent when their five-year-old announced he needed to go too; he wanted to see what dead was.

The family decided to take him before visiting hours and were dismayed when he insisted on wearing his camouflage jeans with the large patch pockets on the pant legs. After much discussion, he revealed he had a packet of fish food in his pocket so Grandma could take it to heaven and feed his Siamese fighting fish. The fish had died a month earlier. Children have creative ways of integrating their understandings into adult perspectives that need to be respected. (Teachers can also use the loss of a pet to open discussions about loss and grief. Students can quickly relate to such a loss, whether it was their pet or even the pet of their grandparents.)

Complicated Losses

Some cases of complicated grief fit within the definition of traumatic stress. Children who have insecure attachment patterns can be expected to have great difficulty with grieving, especially if they are grieving for a parent or care provider. Grieving the death of a parent or close relative

or friend who dies as a result of a criminal activity greatly co[mplicates]
the grieving process for children. Separating from an important p[erson]
is a painful process, and that process is complicated if there was no solid,
trusting connection. The death of that person means that the relationship will never grow and that longed-for words of affection will never
be heard. In a similar manner, children may struggle with why a parent
"abandoned" their child, now in foster care, a situation that generates
grief on several levels. Children with an incarcerated parent also struggle
with a similar perception of loss.

Family disconnections—when some family members are no longer
connected to the child—tend to contribute to complication of losses. For
example, when a noncustodial or uninvolved parent dies, children may be
confused by the lack of respectful grieving by family members. Children
who have a relative or sibling killed while engaging in illegal activities
can be similarly confused and hold back their grief, sensing it may not
meet approval by other family members or close family friends. Teachers
have a great opportunity in such cases to support children who need to
have their grief respected (Kagan 2004; Levine and Kline 2007).

Another complicated loss occurs if the child's last memory of the person
or object includes a personally violent memory or violent incident. In these
instances, the child tends to shut out the overwhelmingly painful memory.
Unfortunately, when this happens, the grieving process shuts down before
it can begin because the child is attempting to avoid a painful reality. For
children to constructively grieve a violent loss, they must first process the
trauma and be offered an opportunity to transform the memory and separate the memory from the person who has died. For some hurting children,
the help of mental health professionals in this area can be invaluable.

Powerlessness—the sense of having no control over events, circumstances, or life itself—is the thread that unites grief and trauma. Trauma
always represents a loss, generally a loss of security. However, unprocessed trauma can stifle the healthy grieving process, and both traumatic stress and grief need to be attended to and processed well. Children
with unresolved losses and terrors need opportunities to experience comfort and discover their own ability to comfort themselves following the
processing of their traumas (Dougy Center 1999). An excellent place to
find resources for teachers and counselors is the Centering Corporation
catalog, which can be ordered by calling 1-866-218-0101 or going to
www.centering.org.

Magical Thinking

Preschool children usually see death as temporary and reversible. This view can interfere with their long-term healing because it is often compounded by anger and a sense of betrayal when the deceased parent does not return. One way very young children cope is through magical thinking. Magical thinking has long been accepted as a natural process for preschoolers struggling to make sense of an experience or event that is beyond their understanding. In the grief process, young children, who all have minimal power in their lives, may engage in magical thinking to avert feeling even more powerless. For this reason, children may engage in fantasy that gives them the sense that if they "caused" the tragedy, they must have the power to change the outcome or at least prevent it from ever happening again (Fogarty 2000). When a child applies magical thinking to the death of a significant person, he may focus on the remaining parent or caregiver to assure that person won't die too. The child imagines possessing personal power that will assure this, which may be expressed as rigid, even unreasonable control.

Another common example of magical thinking is the belief of young children that they are responsible for their maltreatment at others' hands. After all, if they had been good enough, lovable enough, the abuse would never have happened, and they will make sure it will never happen again by being perfect. This form of imaginary power helps give a sense of control over their severe loss of security and respect. In *The Magical Thoughts of Grieving Children*, James A. Fogarty (2000) suggests that when early elementary children engage in magical thinking as a survival strategy, they are not engaging in the essential grieving process, which means the loss is not addressed and remains improperly grieved.

A child who has witnessed loud and aggressive arguments between her parents, often followed by her father's disappearance from home for several days, has become obsessed with perfection. Her teacher has observed her frequently erasing parts of her assignments and even starting a totally new paper. Her teacher has commented on this action, to which the student has replied that the paper didn't look good enough—it has to be perfect! This child's perfectionism is helping her feel a sense of control over her father's absence; if her paper is perfect, surely her father will come back and never leave again.

Supporting Grieving Children

Children who are grieving a loss simply want to be okay again. The greatest gift to them is an adult in their lives who believes that their return to wholeness will occur. Educators need to support children in this process so the children can begin to understand the loss. Even with the limited time teachers have with students, as caring adults they may be able to help students reach the acceptance stage of loss. Remember, their caring family is experiencing their own grief and may not be emotionally available to the child.

Children can slip in and out of grief. Young children tend to process grief in spurts or intermittently, and it may take months for grief behaviors to appear. It is easy for adults to misinterpret these interludes of relief as a sign the child has forgotten the circumstances or topic. Why bring it up and prompt sadness again? It is also possible he or she may feel anger toward the deceased person, which may be difficult to hear. It is important to take the time to listen to the child in a safe place. Provide a haven for children to work through their confusing feelings. Safety is the key to healing. Safe environments allow youngsters to freely examine memories and feelings without any shame or rejection (Kagan 2004).

The delayed grief of moving became very real for our family some years back. Our grandchild lived with her parents in a snug New York apartment. When she began eating solid foods, her mom wanted her to sit in the high chair, but she preferred her mom's lap, so her mom sang to distract her. The favorite song was "You Are My Sunshine."

Shortly after her first birthday, the family moved to a large house in New Jersey. I was there to help care for her during the chaos, but she wouldn't allow me to touch her. She stared at me as if she were looking a million miles past me while the men cutting marble for the foyer and the carpenter crew were using electric saws in the house. The carpenters stayed five months.

Nearly a year later, she received a book with buttons to push for a song to play. When she pushed the button for "You Are My Sunshine," she began to sob deeply for a long time.

While I can't know for sure, I think perhaps she was grieving the loss of that New York apartment and her cozy sanctuary there.

You may find there are times when a grieving child cannot stay on task and would benefit from some private time. During such times a Safe Room can be very beneficial (see chapter 4). Providing some art supplies might help the child rebuild a sense of equilibrium. It is important to talk with the child about what might help create a more comfortable environment (Levine and Kline 2007).

Despite outward clues of emotional calmness, children may revisit their grief often. Holidays and anniversaries of the loss are often particularly stressful times for several years. Be on the alert, especially close to Mother's Day, when the class might make cards or gifts for mothers. If a child has a deceased or absent mother, this well-intended activity can be very painful, because the natural grieving process involves recalling images and memories of the deceased or inaccessible person or object. Similar care needs to be taken on Father's Day and at any events when family members are included.

Adults and Grieving Children

James Fogarty speaks passionately about how inside the most antisocial and violent teen are unprocessed childhood losses, and he suggests that early childhood educators be particularly attentive to students who may be grieving (speeches by Fogarty attended by author).

Adults can help grieving children by examining their own unresolved grief, losses, feelings, and beliefs. Adults who have not dealt with their own feelings or history of helplessness and sadness are unlikely to be able to help children who are struggling with grief and loss, and may not allow themselves to identify with the child's grief. Teachers and adults who find themselves in this position should certainly seek help in beginning their own healing processes.

When adults are unwilling or unable to respond and respect a child's grief, the child is forced to do it alone, which deepens the sense of loneliness. Many educators and other adults have not had the opportunity to observe other adults interacting with grieving children with compassion, so it is natural to feel uncomfortable when children cry about their loss or process it in other ways. We want children to be happy!

One of the many challenges grieving children face is allowing themselves to express their feelings about the loss or separation. Children, like adults, can be creative about hiding their fears and sense of powerlessness. Combative, acting-out behaviors are common defense mechanisms of grieving children, especially boys. Do not be fooled by their angry behavior (Szalavitz and Perry 2010). Sometimes a child will attempt to be perfect in the desperate hope that the person who has died will return. This situation requires great sensitivity and patience as the child restores belief in self. If a loss is sudden and unexpected, children's sense of helplessness intensifies. This perception of helplessness is caused more by the loss of control than the shock itself. Help children in this situation by offering encouragement, choices, and reassurances. Let them know they are valuable, lovable, and important (Levine and Kline 2007).

Besides the loss of a person or object, children have also lost the vision of the way they thought life would be and how their needs would be cared for. Rather than trying to convince them everything is okay, honor their losses and their need to grieve. Do not talk them out of their grief. They need to grieve the dreams lost by their changed circumstance. And they need encouragement to continue dreaming. New dreams are the key to unlocking their hope. Just as children's expressions of mourning and powerlessness tend to be symbolic, healing strategies tend to be symbolic as well. Art, movement, and play become the symbolic language of grief resolution and empowerment for grieving children (Steele and Malchiodi 2012). See the activities offered in part 2 of this book, which afford grieving children the opportunity to create proactive, metaphorical resolutions. Children who are in deep grief have a strong, natural strength to heal. The adults in their lives need to be supportive of each child's unique healing process.

How Children Present Grief

Denial and Shock: A state of disbelief. The behavioral cues are the following:

- flat emotions
- compliant behavior
- rhythmic movement for emotional release
- clinging to mementos
- being prone to injury
- development of real or imaginary illnesses

Bargaining or Magical Undoing: An internal process of self-talk. The behavioral cues are the following:

- dramatic changes in compliance
- perfectionism
- dedication to something the child thinks will correct or change the reality of what happened

Helplessness, Anger, Despair, and Depression: The physical and psychological expression of grief. The behavioral cues are the following:

- defiance and talking back
- swearing
- tantrums
- fighting and hurting others, self, small animals, or property
- regressing in development
- withdrawal
- guilt expressed through "if only" comments

Resolution and Understanding: A process of letting go of anger and guilt. The behavioral cues are the following:

- being relaxed and at ease
- improved concentration and focus
- talking about the tragedy without becoming agitated

Acceptance, Hope, and Resilience: The decision to go on living. The behavioral cues are the following:

- reflecting on the past and drawing strength from it
- talking about the future
- describing or seeing self in the future

Issues of Loss and Separation

Changes in family structure, dwelling, health, and employment can greatly complicate the grieving process for children.

[handwritten margin note: Denial / Bargaining / Anger / Understand / Acceptance]

Changes in Status: New Sibling

Children of all ages are affected by a new person arriving in their home, whether through birth, adoption, or foster care. To a preschooler, a new sibling can be overwhelming and disorienting, particularly if it follows some other loss experience such as a move, change in caregiver, or change in health status. With the addition of a new child to the family, preschoolers can become terrified that their parents no longer love them. Most children are aware that families replace things when they no longer serve their purpose or are wanted. This idea can prompt children to interpret the new baby as a message that they themselves are no longer wanted or loved. They may feel powerless, rejected, and angry. Behavioral changes may not show up for several months. Children may communicate any troublesome feelings and anxieties through behaviors such as nightmares (which cause them to be tired in school), nail biting, hair pulling, muscle aches, stuttering, irritability, teasing, excessive shyness, excessive possessiveness or excessive generosity, meekness, "grazing" in which they wander from activity to activity, and an inability to engage in real play or learning. Educators and other caring adults should trust their intuition and offer healing activities and soothing support that restore children's sense of empowerment and control over their lives. They naturally rally when given the opportunity to make decisions and create artworks, such as drawings, that depict their sense of a future.

Changes in Home or Residence

Home is the cornerstone of a child's world. Even in homes where emotional and physical safety are not routine, most children claim a room, area, or corner as their space—the place where they feel freer to do their dreaming. Moving, even when it is to a bigger or more deluxe building, and especially when it is to a homeless shelter or other shared housing, is a separation and loss that children may need to mourn. Home to a child is filled with memories, which are woven together with its unique aromas and sounds. These sensory imprints, even those experienced before children can speak, allow them to relax, settle back, and breathe deeply at home. The loss of a familiar and predictable place and the senses attached to it have to be mourned before children can embrace their new dwelling place and rebuild their perceptions of security.

In addition, they are learning new streets and neighborhood routes, new neighborhood codes of status, and turf issues. This is stressful! It is only natural that these feelings of stress and grief can impact children's behavior in school. By providing predictable, consistent routines and guidelines, educators can reinforce the sense of security and stability for children who have recently moved. This helps them use their emotional energy to cope and learn.

A young preschooler, who was friendly and cooperative, suddenly turned aggressive. The staff were dismayed as he hit and bit his classmates on Monday. One of the staff was aware his family had moved over the weekend, and she mentioned the changed behaviors to the parent who came to pick up the boy.

That evening, while the mom was cleaning the old apartment, the dad took the boy over to say good-bye to it. Together, all three of them visited each room to say good-bye, giving special attention to what had been the boy's room. They talked about the spot where his bed had stood and about its now being at their new house, along with all his toys.

To everyone's relief, the next day the friendly, relaxed little boy was once again himself.

As with other issues of grief, seasonal and religious holidays may bring back feelings and memories, in this case of a child's previous home. The child may feel sad or angry again or for the first time—and the feelings may interfere with the child's ability to participate in activities. Offer an alternative activity or encourage the child to identify what he wishes would be different, perhaps through drawing or storytelling.

Changes in School or Center Environments

A change in school or caregiver may be necessary for many reasons. Regardless of the cause, frequent changes can be stressful for children. A natural reaction of children stressed by frequent school moves is to avoid investing energy in new friendships or relationships. Some of that resistance may also be directed toward their new teacher. Children who frequently move are grieving past losses and attempting to avert the future pain and disappointment of again having to say good-bye and separate.

The challenges children in a new education setting face include negotiating school social codes and regulations and adjusting to a teacher's style and expectations. All of these challenges are in addition to the family changes and the circumstances that prompted the move. Like children jealous of a new child in their home, these children can communicate their feelings and anxieties through disruptive behaviors. They may also have outbursts, tattle, be excessively vigilant, or withdraw. Help children new to school by offering them the opportunity to express what they would like to change through drawing or storytelling. *The Peaceful Classroom: 162 Easy Activities to Teach Preschoolers Compassion and Cooperation* by Charles A. Smith is a helpful resource. It is written for preschool teachers but can be used by early elementary teachers as well—simply adjust the activities to match the needs of the children.

Changes in Health or Wellness of Child or Family Member

Childhood health crises and their associated medical care can be terrifying. Suddenly a child's world has changed. In addition to the physical effects of the accident or disease itself, the physical predictability of one's own body has been altered. In spite of repeated, caring explanations by family and medical staff, young children have difficulty understanding why intrusive medical treatment (which to children can feel assault-like) was necessary. The result of such experiences may not surface as behavior changes until months later. Children may struggle with their perception of themselves in their world. This may include a sense of insecurity and memories of powerlessness. Educators can introduce healing activities such as those in part 2 of this book to address these dilemmas.

Changes in the health of a family member can generate similar feelings and behaviors in children. As with other losses, children may grieve the change in family life caused by new physical limitations on a parent, such as no longer being able to play outside together. They may also be afraid of the bewildering array of equipment, such as tubes or needles, seeming to invade their loved one.

Feelings of powerlessness and fear are natural in these circumstances and are often compounded by guilt. Young children sometimes assume they have caused the illness or accident of a parent or sibling by having been angry at that family member. Sometimes children may feign illness in the hope that the illness or injury will be transferred to them and they can become more connected with the family member who is suffering.

Children with such burdens need to have their feelings and conditions respected. A referral for counseling should be considered.

The attention focused on the sick family member can generate ambivalent feelings for children as well. Added to the mix of fear and stress may be jealousy. These feelings may surface as behavior changes in school, because the child trusts the educators and sees the environment shared with them as an emotionally safe place.

Frequent communication with the child's family can provide insight and understanding. By sharing puzzling comments or behaviors, both the educators and the family members will be better able to translate and clarify any misinterpretations by the child.

Changes in Family Makeup and Support

The death or unavailability of a family member, caregiver, or sibling can create a shattering loss for children. Since young children formulate their self-identity through the reflections of themselves by primary caregivers, the loss of one of those caregivers can diminish that opportunity. The death of a sibling can bring the realization that a similar fate is a possibility for any child.

Likewise, the divorce or separation of parents can be debilitating to a child. Memories of bickering, fighting, or perhaps violence leading up to the divorce may compound the feelings of loss and separation and lead to a sense of betrayal. Both of the adults are the child's parents, and loyalty to both becomes confusing if not impossible. These feelings are compounded if the child's mourning process is not compatible with the needs of the custodial parent.

Other family changes can also affect children's sense of stability and their ability to achieve. A parent's reentry into the paid workforce can require profound changes and transitions for children. The loss of employment by a parent or caregiver or the addition of a relative to the household also may have destabilizing effects on behavior in the classroom or center.

Once again, the educational setting may be the only environment in which children can work out these feelings and rebuild a sense of control over their lives. Any activity that addresses powerlessness, loss, or anger can help mourning children heal themselves.

Loss of Self-Worth: If the Situation Is Not Intentionally Addressed

Self-worth depends on a child's opportunities to demonstrate competence, mastery, and industry. When such opportunities are blocked, children are intuitively aware of the lost opportunities and their growing sense of powerlessness. Trusting in their ability to shape their future is essential for children's mental health. Children whose experiences do not include opportunities to develop a sense of control will need to process their anger about perceived unfairness. Such losses of self-worth can be helped by healing activities that address anger, powerlessness, and loss (Badenoch 2008).

Whenever children are shamed at home, at school, or in the neighborhood, they anguish over this personal loss of dignity and integrity. Repeated experiences of shame can destroy children's resiliency and capacity to believe in themselves or their future unless healing and empowering opportunities are available.

All forms of child abuse generate deep shame and loss of self-esteem and innocence. Ridicule and verbal attacks can be almost as devastating as physical or sexual abuse. Physical discipline such as spanking can be equally undermining to children's sense of self-worth (Grille 2005).

Most states have eliminated corporal punishment in public institutions. Many may believe that a teacher or a center should not intervene in a family practice of spanking. But giving children the opportunity to work through the feelings generated by such experiences can help them from feeling helpless or acting violent as an adolescent and adult.

6. Helping Children Build Resiliency

The goal of trauma-informed education is to support children and their families in building or rebuilding security after trauma and tragedy. The ability to respond well to adverse life circumstances is called resilience. Resilience is having the skills to cope with disappointments, frustrations, threats, and disasters and to maintain a purposeful and thriving life. It is the ability to face fears, remain self-regulated, and bounce back (Steele and Malchiodi 2012). Being resilient during and following a traumatic experience can be as challenging as it is essential for sustained growth and development (Szalavitz and Perry 2010). It requires strong self-regulation skills, positive role models, and social supports. Promoting resilience in all children is the ultimate goal for those who work with children, including teachers and families (Cozolino 2013).

Resilience in the face of adversity can be demonstrated in many different ways. Often children and adults who express resilience see themselves making a difference in other people's lives, have the ability to reach out for support when they need it, and are able to focus on the positive aspects of their lives. Empathy and hope from adults can empower resilience skills in children (Brendtro, Mitchell, and McCall 2009). Children who demonstrate resilience are able to maintain an excitement about life and live in the present. They are not restricted by the past or the future and are more able to connect with adults, including their teachers and caregivers, through bonds of mutual trust. They are appropriately self-reliant and believe in their own abilities and futures.

Children's lives are unlikely to ever be free from all chaos and violence, as much as we would like that to happen. How, then, can educators help children build resilience to help them cope with possible tragic or frightening experiences? What kinds of skills will children need to withstand the stresses or tragedies they may encounter?

Providing the Tools for Children's Resiliency

There are many ways educators and other adults can help children build resiliency. Help them learn to do the following:

- express and label all their feelings and sensations
- develop self-regulation
- manage fears disguised as anger
- manage their stress
- solve their problems
- participate in their own safety

Help Children Express and Label All Their Feelings and Sensations

Children's ability to label and own all their feelings and recognize that they are normal is an important step in building resiliency skills and empowers children to move from being a victim to being a survivor. They can use the energy of their feelings and sensations to thrive and grow rather than deny they exist. Stressed children need educators to honor all their feelings in order to build self-regulation and empathy.

See chapter 3 for more on helping children express and label their feelings.

Help Children Develop Self-Regulation

Self-regulation skills are a foundational element of resiliency, allowing children to have a sense of control over their behavior and, by extension, over more of their future. Self-regulation involves the ability to monitor and control one's own behaviors. Self-regulation permits students to practice impulse control, remain focused on learning, and resist aggressive survival reactions. It is the basis for cooperation and friendships; strong self-regulation skills are developed when children experience consistent nurturing relationships (Szalavitz and Perry 2010). The skill also includes expressing empathy, the ability to take the perspective of others. See chapter 3 for more on self-regulation and ideas for teachers.

Help Children Manage Fears Disguised as Anger

Children who have been given the right to honor and accept their strong feelings of anger are now free to build skills for managing those feelings, as opposed to "venting" them or acting on them. Suppressing anger or upset feelings is just as unhealthy as acting out anger. Some children have learned that they should never show any sign of negative feelings, however distressed they may be. Other children have learned, for survival purposes, that the way to respond to another's lack of self-regulation is to react with their own aggression. If they are accustomed to aggression, they may engage in inappropriate verbal or physical behavior in an attempt to cause the chaos with which they are familiar.

Modeling appropriate responses to frustration is the best way to teach students how to manage their strong feelings, which can often stem from a sense of insecurity and fear. This is particularly true when adults are responding to a child's acting-out behavior. Current research indicates that children can benefit from or "absorb" the self-regulation modeled by their teacher and environment, especially when a caring adult has taken steps to explain the child's trauma-based responses and help the child feel safe (Steele and Malchiodi 2012). Children's fears should be taken seriously—making fun of them will only intensify the distress. Subjective, intangible fears are very real for young children. Adults need to use imagination and creativity to help children master these fears. The goal is to build perceptions of safety that will harness fears rather than forget or deny them.

How adults guide the process of managing strong emotions will depend on the student's developmental stage. Preschool children can benefit from opportunities to confront fierce monsters or gigantic dragons through stories and symbolic play. Elementary students can begin to master their fears in a more direct and personal manner through art and literacy skills (Levine and Kline 2007). Guide children in rethinking and reworking their beliefs and behaviors by naming the child's feeling and asking questions. Some questions in a conversation might include these examples:

- I see you seem to be very upset. Tell me where you sense that stress in your body.
- Would you like to be able to change that sensation?
- I wonder what you might be able to do for yourself to feel stronger and safer.
- What might you do starting right now to make that possible?

Encouraging children to decrease their sense of powerlessness through actions or exercise is another way to help them manage their behavior. There are many simple activities that can work:

- jumping rope
- stomping up and down the stairs
- pushing their feet down on the floor with great strength while sitting
- stretching or exercising to music
- pounding pegs
- rhythmic movements, such as dancing, stomping, and marching
- sports that do not involve direct physical contact, such as swimming, gymnastics, and martial arts

Help Children Manage Their Stress

Uncertainty, pressure, and competition abound, even for young children, in their home, school, and neighborhood. Some children place an inordinate amount of pressure on themselves for academic achievement. Others endure stress from their parents' expectations. Tension and pressure can also come from a child's sports, recreation, and entertainment—such as too much overstimulating TV, movies, or video games. Loneliness can also be a significant factor in children's anxiety and stress. The sense that they may be shamed or rejected is a cause of great stress for students. The greatest stress children may face is generated by emotional insecurity and the lack of safety, especially if their very existence is at risk due to violence at home or in their community.

Children's worries need to be taken seriously. Children need to have time and support to express, release, and, when possible, resolve their stress. As with other issues addressed in this book, this process can happen only when children trust the adult offering support. Structure and predictability can give children who live in chaos a chance to learn to trust. One way to guide children toward managing their stress is to give them opportunities to shape their experiences while they are at school. Many activities in part 2 of this book can help students explore and reframe stressful situations or thoughts. There are also many simple physical actions children can do, such as stretching, tensing and relaxing muscles, and doing breathing exercises to help them manage stress. Coping skills and strategies to reduce tension that are learned in the preschool and early elementary school years can last a lifetime. Here are some examples:

- Stretching: Have the children pretend to grow from a little, curled-up baby into a great big giant.
- Tensing and relaxing muscles: Have the children tense and relax their muscles like a machine that warms up all its parts, one at a time.
- Breathing exercises: Have the children breathe in warm, comforting air and imagine sending it to every part of the body.

Help Children Solve Their Problems

One way to build resiliency in children is to help them develop their problem-solving skills. Children who trust their problem-solving skills can face the uncertainties of their futures with greater self-confidence and hope. Encouraging children to explore and practice their problem-solving skills will help them begin to manage and trust in their own abilities. Adults also have influence over the sense of safety that the children's environment conveys. Empowering children to brainstorm and generate alternative solutions will only be successful if they trust the emotional security of their environment and their teacher. They need to know they will not experience shame or humiliation for picking the wrong answer or coming up with an outlandish solution. This is essential, whether the child is in a classroom, hallway, cafeteria, car, bus, playground, or school office or on a field trip.

When practicing problem solving, children need to be offered real, manageable choices to help them gain confidence and learn from their mistakes. Certainly the choices offered have to be within the scope of safety and should be ones the adult can afford to offer. By contrast, if adults expect blind obedience to all commands to children, then their only options are obedience or disobedience, which may be necessary at times but do not lead to empowerment and problem-solving growth. Especially in the case of children who are recovering from stress or trauma, expectations of blind obedience can bring perceptions of insecurity and powerlessness.

Similarly, children with perfectionistic tendencies may need opportunities to fail. Failures are an important part of the learning process and do not label the child as a failure. Instead, in manageable doses and with adult support for recovery, learning how to cope with failure can lead to growth (Brendtro, Mitchell, and McCall 2009). Problem solving is less about finding the "right" solution and more about helping children navigate the process and trials of large and small problems.

Guide children toward solutions by asking open-ended questions:

- What would you like to have happen differently?
- What do you see happening that could make that possible?
- What could you do to bring about the change?

Help Children Participate in Their Own Safety

Many children are growing up in a violent society. For some, their very survival may depend on their ability to manage their own safety. The school environment may be the only place in which these skills can be learned and a child's intuition about his own safety can be affirmed (Kagan 2004).

Help children recognize and respect the physical clues their bodies give them to alert them to something unsafe. Those clues can include fast breathing, heavy heartbeats, tummy rumblings, clammy hands, a lump in the throat, or tingling sensations up the back and on the arms (Levine and Kline 2007). All children will have sensed some of these, perhaps while watching a movie. The key is children's response to these signals. If they have been told feeling fear is weak, they will learn to discount the clues and ignore the warnings. Children who have been urged to *always* obey adults may suppress appropriate warning signals even in a situation with an unsafe adult. Teaching children to listen to the body's warning signals about an unsafe person or situation will decrease their chances of becoming a victim of a dangerous situation.

Teachers and other caring adults can empower children to believe in their ability to stay safe. Ask them what they can do to help keep themselves safe, since adults may not always be available. Affirm that children have the right to say no whenever a situation is confusing or they do not feel comfortable.

Assist children in learning how, when, and where danger starts. Ask them questions to get them to think about their safety: What are your first body clues that something may be wrong? What can you do when you feel those body clues? Can you run, make noise, or yell? (Levine and Kline 2007).

Teachers can open conversations with children regarding their need to tell someone about their worries. They can say, for example, "There are times when a child is troubled by a confusing situation and may not know who to talk to about it. Always remember, there are caring adults in our school who are prepared to listen and willing to help."

PART TWO

Classroom Activities for Empowerment

Trauma-informed education is about bringing hope and confidence back to students and those who care for them. It attempts to translate the insights learned from scientific research into activities that can help make a child's world look inviting and manageable again. It is about empowering children to understand the recent past and the present in order to reach for the future. Intuitive teachers know when students are struggling with events beyond their control. They should trust their insights and provide the catalyst: an activity for healing.

Experiences that can be traumatic for youngsters are not always immediately recognized by adults as a source of fear or loss. The key for a child is how the event was interpreted (Perry and Szalavitz 2006). For example, an adult knows that medical treatments serve an important purpose. To a young child, medical treatments can be bewildering and frightening.

Children are capable of doing their own internal processing and healing—with support from caring adults. Adults don't heal children, but adults can provide children with the tools to heal themselves. The silent "aha's" followed by deep exhaling are personal and private and need to be respected as such. Group discussions are advised only when initiated by the student and when they are comfortable for the adult.

Educators will find that introducing healing activities adds very little to their responsibilities. Adults generally do not lead or manage the process or activity. The students themselves directly manage their own internal processing and recovery. For some students, fear has destroyed hope, which is terrorizing. Engaging in activities that permit youngsters to address unresolved developmental issues can help them make some sense out of frightening memories. Through their imaginations, students can change the way the people in their memory act and react, which can be empowering. By creating alternative outcomes through physical play or mental exercises in art and language, students can regain a sense of control over certain past events and begin to believe in their future (Kagan 2004).

The activities for healing and recovery in this book are intended to be used by adults to guide children into self-directed understanding and processing of experiences and memories. They are not intended to glean personal disclosures or to gather information about a child's relationships.

Each activity lists how to do the activity, what issues it is designed to address, the purpose of the activity, and the materials needed. The issues might be readily observable in some children and not apparent at all in others; however, the activities will be helpful for most children in today's complex world. The activities do not have recommended ages; instead, you should rely on your judgment. In general, most activities are appropriate for ages four and up; however, a child's developmental stage is often a better guide to whether an activity is appropriate, and developmental stages do not always correspond with expected ages.

The activities are grouped into categories: healing play, healing arts, and healing language arts. Offering art projects, stories, or puppet plays can make connections with frightening memories and provide opportunities for students to work through unresolved trauma. All of the activities are designed to help students address their personal issues of loss, separation, rejection, fear, despair, frustration, anger, and powerlessness. Introducing these activities offers students the opportunity to understand situations and experiences that may have been confusing and beyond their control. This recovery process allows them to let go of those memories and move forward with their cognitive, social, and emotional development (Levine and Kline 2007).

A few months after the terrorist attacks on September 11, 2001, I presented at a public elementary school. After the morning presentation, the guidance counselor showed me a bulletin board put up by one of the kindergarten teachers. It was close to Valentine's Day, and the board was decorated with lots of red and pink hearts.

The art on display was examples of the kindergarten children's assignment to draw a picture of a helpful machine of their imagination. Ten of the twelve drawings were described to their teacher as machines that would stop violence, keep the bad guys out, or keep children safe. What had amazed their teacher was that the children had never talked about the events on 9/11 or the fear that event had generated in them or their families. Because only sensory actions such as the hand movements in drawing can connect with the memory stored in the amygdala, the key to unlocking their traumatic stress from 9/11 was their drawing.

Choose activities based on the students' developmental skills. Children who have not mastered printing or writing skills may find the play and art activities more productive. Younger children can also benefit from the language arts activities with some adaptations on the adult's part, such as dictating words, using drawing instead of writing, and other creative ideas. Also, there is no age after which these activities cannot be used since their purpose is to promote emotional healing and growth. An older student may have to backtrack to the developmental stage at which the traumatic experience occurred. The healing play activities are natural for preschool groups and can be useful to older children too (Steele and Malchiodi 2012). Play therapy is very valuable in a one-on-one setting, and leading a play activity with an entire classroom can be tricky, as one child's reaction to the activity can set off another's trauma reaction. Teachers should use their knowledge of the children to determine if activities are best implemented directly with a child within the context of a classroom project.

It was Wednesday morning, the most enjoyable part of the week for second grader Anthony, the day his friend from Paws for Reading visited his classroom. Normally Anthony had great difficulty focusing on the printed lines on the page of the book he was reading. Having Diamond, a black Labrador, calmly lie down right beside the beanbag chair he was sitting in helped Anthony relax and focus. Other than licking Anthony's ear three times, Diamond stayed perfectly calm and still and allowed Anthony to feel secure and capable. Children are very comfortable with calm dogs, as dogs never judge.

Many of these activities can also provide an opportunity for elementary students to engage in positive, productive alternatives to acting-out behaviors before they become permanent patterns. It can help to present the activities in the context of remembering how it felt to be a small child, and not to be concerned about doing an activity correctly. Current news events may also provide a meaningful link between submerged memories and reality.

It is an exhilarating experience to stand back and watch children engaged in a healing activity work through their beliefs of powerlessness and hopelessness. The children's faces and eyes will show that they are taking steps toward hope and resiliency.

None of the activities will be counterproductive or a waste of time for those students who are not specifically in need of healing. They all provide developmental or learning enhancements. This eliminates the need to identify, label, or separate children who have a possible need for healing. The activities are neither a regimen nor a recipe for behavior management. They represent an opportunity for renewed hope and a sense of future.

One caution to note: These activities are not intended to place teachers in a counselor or therapist role. Some students may need to be referred for assessment or individual counseling following the use of these activities. However, not all parents carry through on referrals for their children. If this happens, work with parents in a respectful manner to ensure the child receives any additional support that is needed.

7. Healing Play

Every child has the potential for developing self-confidence and positive self-esteem. However, some children have had experiences that have closed down their access to that potential. Confusing or frightening experiences that traumatize young children rob them of their personal power, creating a sense of powerlessness. Choices and options seem to be nonexistent. There is just silent shame.

Healing play can help with this. Healing play is play through which children project their internal world onto toys or through role-playing. Children displace their feelings, wishes, or trauma and symbolically play out their experience in an attempt to understand and make sense out of the memory. Healing play helps build neural networks that repair trauma (Levine and Kline 2007) and strengthen self-regulation skills (Steele and Malchiodi 2012).

A goal of healing play is to nudge children into problem solving and strengthen their abilities to make good choices. This healing is empowering and integral to reinstating hope (Brendtro, Mitchell, and McCall 2009). Trauma-informed teachers understand that for hurting children to develop and trust their ability to solve problems and shape their futures, they must believe they can. Believing in their potential may be the greatest gift educators can give to their students.

Children who are hurting may lack the language skills that would allow them to tell adults how they see their world and themselves. They may have difficulty using words to define or describe their feelings or needs. Spontaneous play may be the most natural vehicle for self-expression. Play is the nonverbal narrative and symbolic language of a traumatic memory. Play is the natural process of talking without talking (Steele and Malchiodi 2012).

Healing play is a natural and normal activity for young children. After all, play is a learning tool for children everywhere and is appropriate for elementary and preschool classrooms. Through healing play, children can begin to discharge feelings and develop new understandings of the experience and their memories of it. Through symbolic play, children can transform the helplessness they have experienced into personal powerfulness. Healing play certainly will not change the outcome or reality of the original frightening event, such as injury or death, but it can provide children with a developmentally meaningful way to process, accept, or tolerate the memory.

By making the learning space a safe environment for expressing feelings and sensations through words and activities, educators can give children the opportunity to work through their defenses and memories. To take such emotional risks and start the recovery process, however, fragile children must have freedom from rejection, ridicule, or shame (Levine and Kline 2007).

Transformation from pain to healing takes place when children actively confront the memories locked within themselves. Issues or topics that are never talked about can remain submerged and corrosive for years. Healing play activities provide a symbolic way to address memories and enable children to process the memories and redirect their impulsive energies more constructively into developing resiliency (Steele and Malchiodi 2012).

To bring up frightening experiences and reopen wounds may seem uncaring and harsh to many adults even when it is done symbolically. It can be awkward at first, especially if the adult has unresolved issues that are similar to what the child is healing from. It is important to know that children yearn to put confusing issues to rest. They want to understand and let go of the bothersome memories. Just as they can heal the scrapes on their knees, in most cases they can heal their beliefs and develop hope for the future.

Children who have witnessed brutal violence may need to repeat or reenact that aggressive act with toys. Acting out a brutal scenario using toys on toys is often a clue that a child has witnessed a disturbing event. Fantasy aggression is not real aggression. Difficult as it may be for adults to observe this form of play, it is essential for healing to take place and needs to be allowed. Telling the child such play is inappropriate will certainly shut down the play (Perry and Szalavitz 2006).

Adult supervision during play is essential to assure physical and emotional safety for everyone in the room. It may be helpful to define boundaries without shutting down the symbolic play process. For example, say, "All of us in this room need to be safe and have our own feelings."

Traumatized children often compulsively repeat a specific play pattern that is related to their confusing or frightening experience. Children can remain stuck in a repetitive play pattern for months, even years, never finding relief or moving toward a resolution. The adult's role is to guide the child toward a reworking of the experience being played out in order to modify or change the outcome (Szalavitz and Perry 2010). Traumatized children locked into compulsive play patterns can benefit from having a calm, caring adult ask open-ended questions that nudge the children toward an alternative resolution of the situation they are reenacting. Problem-solving questions and wonderings, like the ones that follow, can help children move toward a healthier play outcome. Through healing play, children can transform the helplessness they experienced into a proactive, symbolic powerfulness. Such questioning also encourages the children to use the part of their brains that may be undeveloped beyond the fight-or-flight instinct.

Children do not need to respond orally to these questions and wonderings. Their answers will be seen by changes in their behaviors as their stress is reduced.

Questions to Facilitate Healing Play

- What happens next?
- I wonder what the teddy bear hopes will happen next.
- I wonder what the teddy bear wishes would happen differently.
- I wonder what the teddy bear means by that.
- I wonder what it means to be mad/sad/scared.
- I wonder what the teddy bear wishes would change.
- And then what?

- Tell me, could it have been worse?
- I wonder if the doll likes to feel that way.
- What is the doll going to say now?
- And then how will the doll feel?
- I wonder what the toy could do differently.
- What does the toy want to say?
- What's the best thing that could happen?
- How does the toy want to feel?
- I wonder why the toy would do that. What do you think?
- Is the teddy bear afraid something will happen?
- What is it that the teddy bear doesn't like?
- Why do you think the teddy bear does that?
- Can you tell me, is the teddy bear scared or mad?
- Well, it's okay for the teddy bear to be angry. What might the teddy bear be able to do about it?

Healing play needs to be child directed throughout the play experience. Adults do not lead, criticize, or interpret it. Rather, adults are the catalyst for such play and can facilitate its direction toward an alternative outcome for the child. Some emotionally fragile children, however, may not be able to play, because they are preoccupied with survival issues and the violence that swirls around them. They may first require assurances that they are safe and worthy of being comforted. To make progress during healing play, they may need a trusting relationship with the attending adult and a transitional object or toy.

The adult may find opportunities to privately and gently assist children in altering their misunderstanding or distortions regarding the frightening memory. When these opportunities arise, try not to talk children out of their beliefs; rather, move them toward a greater understanding of the event and its memory through problem-solving questions.

If at all possible and the parents or guardians are open to questions, the adult should consult with the child's parents or guardian about any insights they may have about the child. Sometimes parents and guardians interpret another adult's questions about the child's trauma needs as an accusation of wrongdoing by them. This may be a very delicate bridge to cross. The parents or guardians may have vital information and be better positioned to clarify perceptions. Building and maintaining their trust are vital to the child's recovery and continued development.

Although healing play is child directed, there are specific ways adults can support and facilitate the play toward constructive resolutions for young children. Again, the goal is not to elicit direct verbal responses from children but to enhance the processing of their memories or perceptions and support them in moving forward toward empowerment. As tempting as it may be, adults cannot suggest any changes in the actual outcome of the original tragedy. The event, regrettable or sad as it may be, is completed and over. It is important to support children as they learn to deal with the reality of their world (Levine and Kline 2007).

To provide the "tools" for the symbolic replay of traumatic memories, play areas should include toys, props, and settings that match the child's real living environment (Gil 1991). Environments that support healing play may need to reflect any negative but realistic settings that match children's daily experiences and surroundings. For example, in a front porch setting, a bench or rocking chair probably should not appear brand-new and unused. A worn stuffed sofa or a section of picket fence in ill repair may realistically represent the child's experiences and provide comfort.

Witnessing violence within the family is a first lesson in aggression and powerlessness for many children, so it is important to have toys to support children's reenactment of the events that have generated traumatic memories. Toy sets of family figures representing the diversity of the community can become props for replaying family dynamics. Animal family sets serve equally well. Tongue depressor puppets, which depict family members or family roles, are inexpensive to make and are appealing to young children. Tongue depressor puppets of community service people can complement family characters for more complex play. Firefighters, police officers, emergency teams, doctors, and nurses are some examples.

Issues of power, dominance, and powerlessness are central to many frightening memories. Toys that depict various power levels and sizes can provide opportunities to work through these dilemmas. Friendly dinosaurs, dragons, monsters, elephants, and lions are favorites of all children because they combine great size with the capacity to protect and care. At the opposite end of the scale, insects and baby animals are enticing tools for working through size and power issues with preschoolers.

Toy telephones can provide a young child a safe way to talk through events or experiences and create outcomes more to the child's choosing.

Imaginary conversations can become an effective way to discharge energized feelings through words without directly harming anyone.

Providing toys that match what children encounter in their lives can create a dilemma when it comes to allowing toy guns to be used. Children bringing toy guns, knives, and other instruments of violence to the classroom creates difficulties for preschools. For a school or teacher to provide such toys is usually inconceivable. But not all young children have healthy environments and constructive experiences. The decision to provide toy versions of instruments of violence for symbolic healing play requires frank and extensive discussion by all staff members. The final decision needs to be a personal choice based on a full understanding of all the risks and consequences without framing a child's need for protection as unacceptable.

ACTIVITY 1

Tell the Telephone

Materials

unconnected real or realistic toy telephones

Procedure

Encourage children to tell the telephone their needs and wishes whenever they want to. Explain that it is important for them to express their secret desires and any worries they have. Be sure to explain that although their wishes and hopes are important to state, expressing them will not change what has happened. Explain to them that adults and children often feel better after talking about their needs or worries.

Issues

emotional insecurity, separation, loss, a need to be cared for

Purpose

To provide an opportunity for children to anonymously and safely express their needs and hopes.

The Wish Box

Materials

brightly decorated box with a hinged lid, covered by a mirror on the inside

paper

crayons

Procedure

Encourage the children to draw pictures of wishes or hopes that are important to them and place them in the Wish Box. Explain that if they take special care to look at the inside of the lid, they will see a special person who will always be with them while they think about ways to make the wish work out.

Issues

emotional insecurity, separation, loss, a need to be cared for and valued

Purpose

To provide an opportunity for children to express needs and hopes and recognize the one person (themselves) always available to them for meeting their needs.

ACTIVITY 3

Hide and Find

Materials

favorite stuffed animal

Procedure

Encourage one child at a time to hide a stuffed animal or other favorite toy somewhere in the room. Then have the same child look for it and celebrate finding it. Model for the children the caring language and gestures they might use. Affirm each child's personal celebration.

Issues

separation, loss, emotional insecurity

Purpose

To create opportunities for children to experience the joy of reuniting.

ACTIVITY 4

Seeing the World through Colored Glasses

Materials

Make cardboard frames four inches by eight inches with large open centers.

Tape colored cellophane to the frames.

Have students pass the frames so every student can use at least four colored frames.

Procedure

Give the children cardboard frames covered with various colors of cellophane, and encourage them to look through the different colors. Discuss how people and items look different through the colors but actually look the same without the colored cellophane. Introduce and explain that the statement "looking at the world through rose-colored glasses" means everything looks bright and hopeful. Consider these questions for discussion: How might people use their imagination to change the way a place looked and how they felt about it? Looking through what colors might make a place look safe? Comforting? Peaceful? Relaxing?

Suggestions

Offer the colored frames when students ask to repeat the activity.

Issues
insecurity, inability to self-regulate

Purpose
To increase sense of security, being able to manage different environments.

ACTIVITY 5

The Lonely Puppy

Materials
soft stuffed puppy
chart paper and markers

Procedure

Tell the story of a puppy who had been passed by at the dog shelter repeatedly. No one ever smiled at him, yet he really wanted to belong to a family. Finally, a family took him home. There were so many noisy people in the house, the puppy crawled under a bed to hide and feel safe. He didn't eat for two days.

Then say, "What do you think the puppy needed/wanted? I'll write your answers on the board. Let's make a long list." Ask questions like the following:

- What was the puppy feeling inside?
- What might you all give the puppy to help him feel safe and comfortable? Each of you will be handed the puppy to demonstrate how you would handle him so he would feel safe and secure. How would you talk to the puppy so he could feel calm and loved?

Then say, "Now I would like each of you to draw a picture of the puppy when he felt safe and happy."

Issues
insecure attachment, uncooperativeness, insecurity

Purpose
To grow empathy and a sense of belonging.

ACTIVITY

6

Flubber

Materials
white school glue
water
food coloring
borax
fork or spoon for stirring
mixing bowl
watercolor markers, for the variation

Procedure

Make flubber with the children:

- Mix two cups of white school glue into two cups of water along with food coloring of your choice.
- Add two tablespoons of borax to one cup of warm water in a separate cup, and stir until dissolved.
- Add this mixture to the glue and colored water mixture, and stir with a strong spoon or fork.
- Mix several times, cover, and set aside until the next morning.
- Mix again or even knead until all liquid is integrated. Cover and store. It does not need refrigeration.

Variations
Do not add food coloring, and instead provide watercolor markers and allow children to draw on the white flubber; then mix the colors by kneading the flubber.

Suggestions

Provide the premade flubber when children need a calming sensory activity.

Issues

physical insecurity, emotional insecurity, feeling tense and agitated

Purpose

To provide an opportunity for children to engage the sense of physical touch and practice self-calming.

ACTIVITY 7

Rescue Teams

Materials

toy animal
sheet or blanket
wide ribbon or rope, for the variation

Procedure

Tell the children a story about a little kitten who gets lost and is found. Here is an example:

A little kitten gets lost under a thick cluster of bushes. A group of children walking home from school hear the kitten's scared- and lonely-sounding meows. The children decide to form a rescue team by linking their hands one to another and carefully inching the first child under the bushes to rescue the kitten. The first child passes the kitten down the rescue chain to the next child. From hand to hand, each child comforts the kitten with soft words and gentle strokes.

When finished, invite the children to discuss their feelings about the story. Later, act out the story. For example, drape a sheet or blanket over a low table, and place a toy animal under the table. Guide groups of about four or five children in becoming a rescue team for the toy animal.

Variations

Tell the same story as in the first procedure, then assist children in forming rescue teams to come to the aid of a "lost" or separated child. Create a divide by placing a ribbon or rope on the floor. Have the rescue team lead their classmate to safety amid greetings of joy and caring. Repeat as needed.

Suggestions

Ask the children who could become a rescue team for them if they ever need one at home or in their neighborhood.

Issues

physical insecurity, emotional insecurity, a need for safety and protection

Purpose

To help children start to overcome their fears.

ACTIVITY 8

Care Wrapping

Materials

large stuffed toy or doll

stretchable bandages (such as ACE bandages) cut into two-foot lengths

masking tape

Procedure

Explain to the children that a toy or doll has fallen and injured its arm or leg and hurts. Using comforting words, carefully and gently apply the bandage, securing it with masking tape.

Variations

Using yourself as an example, ask a child to volunteer to bandage your arm. Ask children to form teams of three, and taking turns, have one child pretend to be injured and the other two act as caregivers.

Issues

emotional insecurity, a need to be comforted or cared for

Purpose

To provide opportunities for children to discover their capacity to care for others and help themselves at the same time.

ACTIVITY 9

Mother Hens

Materials
large fans or scarves

Procedure

Tell the children a story about a mother hen whose little chicks have no feathers to protect themselves from the rain. During the story, use fans or scarves as simulated wings, and show how the mother hen would use them to protect her chicks. As you repeat the story's details, add sound effects of the mother hen clucking. Have the children make the sounds of the chicks peeping as they seek shelter and protection.

Ask the children to form groups of five or six, and give each group two fans or scarves. Designate who in each group will play mother hen, and have the groups perform the story. Repeat, allowing each child to have a turn as mother hen providing safety and protection by holding up or spreading out the fans as make-believe wings.

Suggestions
Discuss the children's feelings about the story. Ask these questions: What did it feel like to be protected? How did it feel being the mother and protecting others?

Issues
physical insecurity, emotional insecurity, a need to be protected

Purpose
To provide an opportunity for children to protect others and help themselves at the same time.

ACTIVITY 10

Growing Empathy

Materials

A visit from an infant and her parent, or alternatively a baby doll

baby blankets

Procedure

Talk to the children about caring for infants. Ask them these questions: Have any of you ever watched an adult care for a new baby? How did you know the baby felt safe and secure? How would you describe the way the adult held the baby? How did the adult talk to the baby?

Offer each child an opportunity to hold the baby in the most caring way possible and use the soothing words and voice that would comfort the baby.

Issues

distrust, insecurity, limited impulse control

Purpose

To provide an opportunity for children to strengthen their capacity for empathy and to allow students to discover their ability to be caring.

ACTIVITY 11

Big and Little Lions

Materials

paper or cardboard crowns

music

Procedure

Discuss that lions are often called the king of beasts and what that means—powerful, courageous, and fierce. Then talk about lions being parents with little lion cubs to care for and protect. Explain that they have to be tender and gentle at the same time they are powerful and fierce. Wearing a crown to pretend you are a lion king, demonstrate gentleness by giving a gentle hug to each child. Be sure to ask each child if you may hug him. Discuss what it means to be gentle.

Since this game involves hugging, do not force children into roles. Ask the children to choose to be huggers or watchers. Being a watcher is a good role for children uncomfortable with giving or receiving hugs. They can be acacia trees. The huggers will be lions. Give crowns to half the lion children, who will be lion kings, and ask the other half to be lion cubs. With music playing, have the children walk about the space growling or meowing according to their role. When the music stops, the lions should gently hug.

Suggestions

Play the first round as described. For each additional round, give out more crowns, adding to the number of lion kings, creating bigger and bigger hugging bunches, until finally everyone participating is a lion king, hugging each other gently.

Issues

vulnerability, a need to trust and be cared for

Purpose

To provide an opportunity for children to experience and practice being gentle and powerful.

ACTIVITY 12

Becoming a Helper Friend

Materials

chart paper and marker

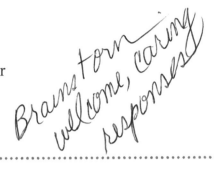

Brainstorm welcome, caring responses

Procedure

Ask the children if they were ever in a class that had a new student join during the school year. Ask them things like, How did you feel when the new student entered your class? Did you feel the same way a month later? What helped you change your attitude, if that happened? Write their responses on the chart paper.

Next, help the children think about how the new student felt: What do you imagine the new student was feeling? What might he have been sensing in his throat? In his chest? In his stomach? Write their responses on the chart paper. Then ask, What do you think the new student had hoped he would experience his first days in your class? Say, Let's list the personal characteristics or behaviors the new student had hoped he would like to observe in a classmate who would befriend him and help him feel welcome and respected.

Have children pick a partner and greet one another in the way the new student hoped to be treated. Discuss with them how that felt.

Issues

uncooperativeness, name-calling, rejection of some classmates

Purpose

To provide opportunities for children to strengthen their capacity for empathy and to discover their abilities to be helper friends.

ACTIVITY 13

Magic Wands of Courage

Materials

plastic drinking straws
large gold stickers
strands of curling ribbon
stapler
variety of toy animals

Procedure

Demonstrate how to make wands by stapling a large gold sticker and several strands of curling ribbon to one end of a straw.

Tell the children a story about two lost bunnies and a magic wand. Here's an example:

Two little bunnies were having such a good time playing that they paid no attention to where they were hopping. Suddenly they heard a noise they did not recognize and were very frightened. They looked around and realized they did not recognize one single tree or bush and did not know which way to hop to get home. They were lost.

They became so fearful, they were frozen and could not move. Just then, a squirrel climbed down from a tree above them and waved a Magic Wand of Courage in front of them (*demonstrate*). The squirrel asked them questions to help them.

The squirrel asked, "Did you hop past the fence that's over there?" (*point toward an imaginary fence*). "Did you hop past the gently swooshing fir tree that's over there?" (*point in another direction*). "Did you hop past the apple tree that's over there?" (*point in yet another direction*). The bunnies, who were now completely unfrozen, thought over the questions and remembered passing the apple tree. They joyfully hopped in that direction, past the tree.

Discuss how using our thinking powers can help us find solutions and feel confident. Ask the children if the wand brought the solutions or if the questioning and thinking did.

Help the children make their wands.

As a group, consider similar situations of fear of being lost with toy animals that have been selected and placed around the room. Have the children use their Magic Wands to help each animal build the courage needed to stay safe. Have them ask the toy animal questions such as these: How could you feel safer? How could you find your way back to safety?

Suggestions

Encourage the children to use imaginary Magic Wands of Courage to help them use their thinking powers and their courage in situations such as losing sight of a parent in a store, hearing surprising noises, or not remembering where the house key is.

Issues
fear, a need to feel courageous

Purpose
To build courage by allowing children to appreciate and respect their fears while learning they can confront them.

ACTIVITY 14

Hands of Courage

Materials

pictures of situations or objects that could be dangerous to young children, such as the water's edge, ladders, campfires, or lawn mowers

collection of gloves and mittens

Procedure

Talk about issues of danger and safety with the children, including the importance of thinking through ways to stay safe and being courageous. Show pictures of situations or objects that could be dangerous to the children, and discuss why they may be dangerous.

Have the children figure out how they can help a younger child confronting the danger in the pictures. Ask them what words they could use so the other child would not panic.

Pass out gloves and mittens, telling the children they now each possess symbolic "Hands of Courage." Discuss how they can imagine wearing the gloves during times when they need protection. Have children explain how they might use their imaginary Hands of Courage to rescue a young child in one of the situations they have just discussed, and how they would bring the child to safety. Repeat as necessary, using different situations or pictures.

Issues

physical insecurity, a need for safety and protection

Purpose

To provide an opportunity for children to protect others and help themselves at the same time.

ACTIVITY 15

Meeting Nightmares

Materials

paper

tape

pencils or crayons

backpack, suitcase, or briefcase (optional)

Procedure

Tell the story of a girl who packed a suitcase (or backpack) one night before going to bed. She put in boots for the swamp, a flashlight in case the clouds covered the moon, and a bottle of water in case she got thirsty. Her sister, who shared her bedroom, asked if she was running away. She responded, "No, but I'll be ready in case I have another nightmare!"

Encourage children to name items they would find helpful in their suitcase if they were packing one as the girl in the story did for meeting her nightmares. Hand out paper and pencils, and have the children draw the items they would want to bring. Children then can fold the paper in half and tape it shut to represent an imaginary suitcase. If a real suitcase is available, have each child stick his paper in the suitcase.

Note: This activity is based on the delightful book _Sandy's Suitcase_ by Elsy Edwards, which is no longer in print.

Issues

fear caused by nightmares or flashbacks

Purpose

To help children regain power and control over their fears.

Walking Bravely

Materials

wide ribbon or rope

toy puppy

Procedure

Tell the following story:

One day a little girl named Annie was walking her puppy, Edgar, who was sniffing and exploring every bush and tree along the sidewalks. Annie did not notice that Edgar was lagging farther and farther behind her.

Edgar came to a fenced-in yard and was just beginning to sniff at the fence when suddenly a great big dog ran up to the fence from the inside of the yard and barked very fiercely. Edgar was terrified!

Annie turned around to see where Edgar was when she heard the big dog barking, and she was frightened too. Edgar had nervously stopped walking and was whining and yelping. Annie was too afraid to walk back to rescue her puppy.

Ask the children what Annie could do. Encourage suggestions that would keep Annie, Edgar, and the barking dog safe. Offer the suggestion that maybe Annie could sing a song to encourage herself; then sing the following song to the children. It is to the tune of "If You're Happy and You Know It."

> If you're scared and you know it, stop and think.
> If you're scared and you know it, stop and think.
> If you're scared and you know it, it's okay, you can control it.
> If you're scared and you know it, stop and think.

Finish the story by telling the children that when Annie heard herself say the words of the song, she was able to find her courage and walk past the barking dog behind the fence and rescue her puppy.

After telling the story, teach children to sing the song. Ask for volunteers to be Annie, the puppy Edgar, and the big, barking dog. Place a ribbon or rope on the floor to represent the fence. Have every child play the role of Annie—use the child's real name while replaying the story. Repeat as needed.

Issues
physical insecurity, emotional insecurity, a need for safety and protection

Purpose
To help children start to overcome their fears.

ACTIVITY 17

Bells of Courage

Materials

bell (with a handle if possible)

Procedure

Tell the following story:

Long, long ago, in a land far away, there was a happy village of people. The people in the village loved their children and knew that their children's greatest joy was eating fresh blueberries. Blueberries grow wild in the forest, so someone had to go deep into the woods to pick them.

Each summer, the village asked which teenagers would volunteer to pick the blueberries, and each summer a few offered to go into the woods, but none of them ever came back. So one summer, one of the mothers decided to silently follow the teenagers, being careful never to let them see her.

Far, far into the woods, the teenagers found big, delicious berries, which they picked as they wandered deeper and deeper into the woods. They did not watch where they were going or how they had gotten there.

When it started to get dark, they realized they were lost and allowed their fear to freeze them into statues. When the mother saw this, she rang the bell she always carried with her, which surprised the teenagers and woke them from their fear. They used their courage and their strength of mind to follow the sound of the bell and find their way out of the woods.

Ask the children what a rescue team does and when a rescue team would be needed. Talk about imaginary situations that might cause a child to want to be rescued. Have the children act out sample situations and take turns ringing the bell to wake each other from their fears. Help them build their courage by having them act out or talk about their return to safety. Ask them how a child who overcame a fear might feel. Ask how a child can keep a feeling of courage from day to day.

Issues
physical insecurity, emotional insecurity, a need for protection and safety

Purpose
To help children start to overcome their fears. To help students see that a child can be brave and still be scared.

ACTIVITY 18

Releasing Worries and Fears

Worries in a shredder

Materials
balloons
small pieces of paper
writing and drawing tools

Procedure

Encourage the children or an individual child to write or draw worries, fears, or secrets on a small piece of paper. Place the paper into a balloon, blow it up with helium, tie the balloon, then release it into the air. Let the children watch it float away, and imagine their worries going with it. Discuss with the children how this makes them feel.

Variations

Give each child an envelope or small paper bag in which to insert their note or drawing. Close or seal them, and then place them into a larger bag or box. Ask the children to help decide where to send or deliver the collection. <u>Or have each child put his or her worries/fear sheet through a shredder.</u>

Issues
powerlessness, loss

Purpose
To get children to recognize that they can let go of issues they have no control over.

8. Healing Arts

Art activities—which include creative movement—can provide children with meaningful opportunities to process hurtful, traumatic experiences and losses. Healing art activities offer children the chance to put feelings into forms or shapes and release memories and sensations. By providing stimulating art activities for children, adults help them use art to symbolically express preverbal experiences, similar to the way children use healing play (Steele and Malchiodi 2012). The creation of art can be a comfortable process because it allows children to communicate symbolically and get rid of unhappy feelings about incomprehensible experiences and frightening memories. Trauma-informed teachers know that direct inquiry seldom leads to productive understandings. We are all familiar with a child's response of "I don't know!" or a shrug of the shoulders to our questions of "Why?" or "What made you do that?"

Drawing provides children with a safe, nonthreatening opportunity to connect with memories that are confusing or scary. Drawing can tap "frozen" memories to assist in healing (Steele and Malchiodi 2012). Through drawing or the creation of other art forms, children can symbolically work out an alternative outcome or resolution that brings relief from the frightening memory. Often they don't know why they feel the way they do until after they have drawn it. Regardless of their level of language development, traumatized children can relieve themselves from their perceptions of powerlessness and helplessness through drawing and other creative arts.

Children can find healing art a safe way to express experiences and memories without identifying or labeling persons or events. Healing art activities are empowering for children because they can control the event and behavior of others to create a desirable outcome. They can freely connect with their dreams and hopes through expressive art, knowing they alone hold the key to the real meaning of the piece. It becomes a safe, risk-free way to express their needs and desires (Levine and Kline 2007). Healing art activities can give children another way to understand their feelings and learn that feeling bad does not mean that *they* are bad (Cohen, Barnes, and Rankin 1995).

Finally, healing art activities give teachers and other caregivers insights into how children see their world and themselves in that world.

ACTIVITY 19

Coloring Feelings

Materials

variety of colored paper hearts (laminated hearts are an option)

double-stick tape or regular masking tape

Procedure

Post colored hearts on a wall along with a list of suggested meanings for the colors. You may use the list below or encourage children to select their own meanings for the colors.

blue = sad

brown = frustrated

gold = strong

navy blue = scared

pink = jolly or silly

red = ~~happy~~ *angry*

yellow = hopeful, *happy*

blue green = worried

dark green = comforted

green = cooperative

orange = ~~angry~~ *courageous*

purple = betrayed

silver blue = lonely, brittle, cold inside

Encourage the children to wear hearts, when they want, to communicate how they are feeling. The adults in the classroom should also participate. These hearts could be reusable and stored in a special place.

Issues

unexpressed feelings

Purpose

To help children identify, respect, and communicate feelings.

ACTIVITY 20

Drawings for Power

Materials

paper

drawing, painting, and writing tools

Procedure

Invite the children or individual child to draw a picture of one of the following people, places, and situations. Discuss the drawings with the children, asking them to tell you only what they want to about the pictures. Accept what they say, and affirm their right to have and express their feelings. Repeat another time with a different item on the list.

- someone the child can always talk to
- a place where the child can always feel safe
- a scary dream or experience (After drawing it, have the child tear it up and destroy it.)
- the same or another scary dream but adding someone or something that allows the child to feel safer
- someone the child trusts and respects
- someone who trusts the child
- a monster who looks angry, sad, lonely, scared, or happy
- a house or place where the child can feel protected and safe
- a house or place where the child might not feel safe or protected (After drawing it, have the child change the house or place so that it could be safe.)
- a home where the child once lived and would like to see again
- a school or classroom that would be a welcoming, friendly place in which to be

- something the child would like to take from the classroom when the child moves on to a new room or school (If the drawing is an ugly or unpleasant picture, have the child change it so that it is more comfortable or pleasing to the child.)
- something that could be called or titled "anger," "sad," or "scary"
- a wish or hope of how the child wants to feel today
- a mad, scary face (After drawing it, have the child change it to be less scary.)
- a dog the child would like to have as a companion (Please note, if a child is frightened, he will often draw large, fierce dogs. If a child is lonely, she will often draw a small lap dog.)
- a monster protecting a treasure; have the child show how to get past the monster to get to the treasure.
- an animal the child would choose to be for a day

Issues
powerlessness, loss

Purpose
To help children feel, in a positive way, more powerful and in control.

ACTIVITY 21

The Teardrops of My Heart

Materials

precut blue teardrops, at least three by six inches
(The teardrops can be laminated on one side if desired.)
double-stick tape or regular masking tape
writing tools

Procedure

Encourage everyone in the room, including adults, to wear a teardrop over the heart, as needed, for comforting and healing. If they want, they can describe their sadness—in a drawing or written in code—on the back of the teardrop where it faces their heart.

Issues

loneliness, loss, insecurity, fear of rejection

Purpose

To help children learn to express their inner feelings.

ACTIVITY 22

Wishing Rainbow

Materials

red, orange, yellow, green, blue, and purple paper cut into two-and-one-half-by-eight-inch strips

double-stick tape or masking tape

paper for hand drawings that match the students' skin colors

writing and drawing tools

scissors

a large poster board securely hung on the wall

Procedure

Discuss rainbows and what they mean to people. For example, ask if the children think rainbows mean good or bad luck. Ask if they know any songs about rainbows, such as "Somewhere over the Rainbow."

Offer the children strips of colored paper, and ask them to write or draw their dream or hope for comfort and happiness. When they have finished this, arrange the strips to form an arch across the upper portion of the poster board in the form of a rainbow.

Next, use precut hands of skin-colored paper, or ask the children to draw around their hand on the paper and cut out the shape. Encourage the children to think of important wishes or dreams and decide what they might do, starting that day, to make that wish or dream come true or begin to come true. They can draw or write their wish or dream on the hand.

Place their action hand under the rainbow. Allow this to be a long-term, ongoing project as needed.

Issues

hopelessness, powerlessness, loss

Purpose

To connect children with their dreams and wishes and translate them into possible actions.

Color Out All of the Anger and Sadness

Materials
crayons
unlined paper

Procedure

Suggest that children, when they need to, take a red-orange crayon and color out all of the anger within them. Ask if they can feel the anger moving through their arms and hands as it leaves their body and becomes the color on the page.

Suggest that children, when they need to, take a blue crayon and do the same to color out all of the sadness or loneliness within them.

Ask the children what they can do, if they want to, to change their feelings. Ask what color they would color when they feel another person is angry at them. Then ask them what color they would use when they do not allow themselves to get angry when another person is angry at them. Allow children to color with any colors they choose.

Issues
powerlessness, anger, loneliness, loss, sadness

Purpose
To teach children they have the ability to change their feelings and to comfort themselves.

ACTIVITY 24

Coloring Solutions

Materials

crayons
unlined paper

Procedure

Ask the child or children to choose a color that shows how they feel when they do not know how to solve a problem or change an outcome. If they are having a hard time choosing a color, encourage them to think about what it feels like to be blocked from doing something they want to do, and to decide what color would best describe that feeling. Let them color or draw whatever they choose in that color. Then have them pick a color that describes how they feel when they know what they might do in a difficult situation.

Ask the children what they can do for themselves so they can change the way they are feeling. Have them pick a color that represents the new feeling and write or draw in that color.

Ask the children to color the way they might feel or sense inside their head, chest, or tummy when they are hearing words or information they do not want to hear. Then ask them to think about how those feelings can be erased or changed with a new color representing a more comforting feeling. Let them color over the first color with the new chosen color.

Issues
poor problem-solving skills, powerlessness, hopelessness

Purpose
To increase children's problem-solving skills and self-esteem.

ACTIVITY 25

Memory Chains

Materials

colored paper cut into strips one inch wide by eight
inches long
writing tools and glue

Procedure

Ask if anyone has ever made a paper chain. Memory chains are made the
same way.

Encourage the students to think about all the people who have been
kind and helpful to them. Write the first names of those people on one
side of the paper strip, and what they said or did that helped the child feel
cared for and strong on the other side. Glue the ends of the strips together
to make a link through another link.

Issues
need, disconnect

Purpose
To help students realize that we gain strength from loved ones by
holding on to the memories of how they helped us feel safe and
strong.

Caring Coupons

Materials

writing and drawing tools

unlined three-by-five-inch cards, in two different colors, if possible

Procedure

Discuss and explain coupons. What are they used for? By whom? When? Are they free, or does a person have to buy them?

Explain that coupons do not have to be used only at a store and that they can make coupons for "Gifts of Caring" to be used when they need a hug or a smile or to share when they want to give a Gift of Caring. Hand out three-by-five-inch cards, and ask the children to decorate one side and on the other side write the Gift of Caring they choose. For younger children, write the suggestions for Gifts of Caring for them. Encourage them to give the coupons to others at home or school when they want to receive or give a little caring.

If you have two different colors of cards, use one color for giving care coupons and another color for receiving care coupons.

Here are examples of Gifts of Caring to give to others:

I will play with you today.
I will smile at you today.
I will be your special friend today.
I will give you a hug today.
I will sit next to you today.
I will comfort you today.

Here are examples of Gifts of Caring to ask to receive from others:

I need a smile today.
I need a hug today.
I need your friendship today.
I need your comfort today.

Issues
feeling unloved and unlovable, grieving

Purpose
To help children discover their capacity to care for others and help themselves at the same time. To help children practice kindness.

ACTIVITY 27

Portraits of Loving Memorials

Materials

writing and drawing tools

unlined paper or photocopies of picture frames you draw yourself

Procedure

Ask the children to visualize the look of someone or something they long for and miss. Discuss how losing something or someone important can be sad and how people often worry they might lose the memory. Ask them how someone could be certain never to forget that valued person, toy, or pet. Have the children draw a picture of the treasured memory on the unlined paper or on the paper with the frame photocopied on it.

Encourage the children to consider the safest place they could keep their treasured memory. Discuss how they might be able to recall that memory without actually looking at it or having it in front of them. Would they have to look at the picture to remember?

Issues

grief, loss, separation from a loved one

Purpose

To help children learn to comfort themselves.

Portraits of Trust and Friendship

Materials

writing and drawing tools

unlined paper or photocopies of picture frames you draw yourself

Procedure

Have the children draw a picture of someone they trust who also trusts them. When the picture is finished, encourage them to write what they would like to say to or hear said by the person in the picture. Younger children can tell you the words and you can write them.

Issues

a sense of being disconnected, grieving

Purpose

To help children identify and strengthen bonds or attachments.

ACTIVITY 29

Safety Badge

Materials

writing and drawing tools

precut badges you draw yourself on colored paper

laminating materials or clear sandwich bags

masking tape

safety pins

Procedure

Ask the children to think about what they could carry with them to make them feel safe and secure. Give them guidelines on what items would also ensure that others around them are able to feel safe.

After the discussion, give the children precut, colored badges. Ask them to draw or write on their badge the item or idea that makes them feel safe. Offer replacements until they are satisfied with their drawing. For protection and durability, laminate the badges, or place them in plastic sandwich bags and tape shut. Tape the safety pin to the badge, and pin it on the child, or if pins are not available, attach it with masking tape.

Allow the children to wear their badges whenever they feel the need to.

Issues
insecurity, loss

Purpose
To help children develop a sense of security.

ACTIVITY 30

Safety Shields

Materials

brown paper (opened-up paper bags work) or sheets of newsprint

medium-weight cardboard in a variety of colors, if possible, about two feet by three feet, one for each child

writing and drawing tools

strapping tape

sturdy fabric, such as denim, cut into one-by-twelve-inch strips, one for each child

Procedure

Talk about what a shield is and what kind of shield the children would need to feel safe at all times. For example, what might such a shield be made of and what would it look like?

After the discussion, help the children decide the shape of their shield. Use the brown paper or newsprint sheets to make a pattern in the desired shape. Trace or transfer the shape to cardboard, and cut it out. Have the children decorate the shield in a way that represents what it would take to help them feel safe. With the strapping tape, attach the fabric strip to the back side of the cardboard to create a handle.

Discuss with the children how they can pretend to carry and use an imaginary shield, even when it is not with them.

Issues
insecurity, loss

Purpose
To help children develop a sense of security.

ACTIVITY 31

My Own Hero

Materials
sheets of paper
drawing and writing tools

Procedure

Discuss how it is common for children to dream about having their own hero who can help them feel secure, safe, and respected. Discuss what it means to be a hero, strong in heart, body, and mind. Ask the children, "Can brave children or animals ever be scared? Do heroes ever get scared? Would you want a hero that never got scared? Why or why not?"

Give each child a sheet of paper. On one side of the paper, ask the children to draw a picture of the hero of their dreams, be it human or animal. On the other side, ask children to write the personal characteristics or strengths that the hero could use to help them feel safe, secure, and respected.

Issues
disconnection from care providers, insecurity, powerlessness

Purpose
To empower children to be able to accept fears and to accept that the same person can be brave and scared.

ACTIVITY 32

The Healing Garden

Materials

art supplies
unlined paper

Procedure

Talk about the beauty of flower gardens and how flower buds might be thought of as hope and blossoms as joy. Look at artwork and photographs of flower gardens. Explain that most people are not able to be in such beautiful gardens every day, but the children (and adults) can create their own gardens in their imaginations and go there whenever they want. Sit back, close your eyes, if that is comfortable, and dream you are in your imaginary garden. What smells or aromas might you sense? What sounds might you hear there? Would the ground be soft or hard and lumpy?

After the discussion, pass out art materials and have the children draw their idea of a healing garden or a place they could visit in their imaginations whenever they need to comfort themselves.

Variations

Repeat the activity using an enchanted forest or a fresh, running stream as the setting.

Suggestions

Encourage the children to think about whom they would like to invite to visit them in their healing garden.

Issues

hurt, anxiety, insecurity, loss

Purpose

To encourage children to comfort and heal themselves using their imagination.

ACTIVITY 33

A Bad-Dream Catcher

Materials

ten-inch circles cut from cardboard, or hoops of similar size of wood or plastic from a craft store

beads and feathers from a craft store

yarn

Procedure

Tell the class about the American Indian tradition of dream catchers, which are hung above where people sleep. A dream catcher is traditionally made of a small branch bent into a circle and held in place with strings. Strings cross the center of the circle to make a sieve. The dream catcher allows the good dreams to pass through but catches the scary ones, not allowing them to reach children.

While students are making their dream catchers, start a discussion about good dreams and bad ones.

Issues
insecurity, powerlessness

Purpose
To provide opportunities for children to gain a sense of control over bad dreams.

ACTIVITY 34

Dream Family

Materials
art supplies
unlined paper

Procedure

Explain what a foster or adoptive family is. Then tell this story:

A child named Henry, from a land far away, traveled to a new city because his parents had died in an accident. Henry had been told he would live with the Cassidy family on Oak Street. But when he got to the house on Oak Street, no one named Cassidy lived there. So, the grown-ups in the city offered Henry the chance to choose the family of his dreams. Although Henry never forgot his first family, he found ways to be happy with his new family.

Ask the children to consider whom they would have selected as a dream family if they had been Henry. Have them draw a picture of that family. Assure the children the meaning of their picture will remain personal and private to them.

Issues
lack of empowerment or sense of control and connection

Purpose
To help children affirm their right to make choices and have dreams.

ACTIVITY 35

Love Bank

Materials

canister with a lid, such as an oatmeal box—decorate it with the children!

art supplies

red or pink paper hearts about five or six inches big

Procedure

Briefly explain the banking system and the concept of making deposits in order to have money available for withdrawals when needed. Then talk about other types of banks, such as blood banks and food banks.

After the discussion, tell the children they are going to set up a love bank. Explain that the canister will be the bank for their love. Encourage the children to write thoughts of joy or love on the hearts and deposit them in the canister bank. Younger children can draw joyful pictures or color their hearts with loving and joyful colors. Explain that the hearts will stay in the bank for times when someone may need to make a withdrawal.

Establish a procedure that from now on everyone can make a deposit when they have extra good memories and feelings, and they can make withdrawals on days when they need comfort and care for themselves or to give to a friend or classmate.

Issues
emotional insecurity, feeling unloved, disconnection, loss

Purpose
To help children discover their capacity to care for themselves and others.

Caring Blanket

Materials

paper or cloth squares

fabric markers or regular markers

glue and a large sheet of paper (quilt size), or a sewing machine

Procedure

Ask the children if they have heard of blankets that are called comforters or security blankets. Ask if anyone knows what those terms could mean, why someone would want one with either name, and what benefits they might have. Explain that the class is going to make one of these together, and let them decide whether to call it a comforter or security blanket.

Provide each child with a square of cloth or paper and markers. Ask them to decorate their square with the design that represents safety, security, or comfort to them. When each child's square is completed, attach them with glue on a larger sheet of paper or sew together.

Issues

physical and emotional insecurity, fear or memories of being lost, loneliness

Purpose

To recognize children's worries, provide support, and teach them to identify their options.

ACTIVITY 37

Power Hats

Materials

unlined paper or photocopies of familiar occupational hats that you draw yourself

writing and drawing tools

art supplies, as needed

Procedure

Discuss how certain hats worn by people help communicate who the wearers might be or what type of work they do. Talk about the personal characteristics that are often associated with the wearers of some hats: firefighters in their hats are considered brave, park rangers in their hats are considered trustworthy, laborers in their hard hats are considered strong, and graduates in their mortarboards are considered smart.

Discuss the possibility of children empowering themselves with strengths and skills by creating and wearing Power Hats. For example, the children could create any of the following hats or others they think of themselves:

- Thinking Hats
- Courage Hats
- Caring Hats
- Comfort Hats
- Respect Hats
- Contented Hats
- No-More-Anger Hats
- Cooperation Hats

Have each child choose a hat title. Ask the children to think about what they need so that they feel like the hat title they chose—what might they need or want in order to feel courageous, respected, and so forth.

Suggest that children draw a hat with the symbolic items that would help them feel stronger or safer, or use the photocopies of hats you have drawn. Younger children can draw what they like then describe their hats to an adult, who can write the words for them.

The children could make hats out of art supplies like paper, glitter, and scraps. Allow children to wear their hats when they feel it is appropriate.

Issues
powerlessness, loss, insecurity, fear, confusion

Purpose
To encourage children to trust in their problem-solving skills and internal power.

Magic Camera

Materials

old cameras (without film) or toy cameras

paper

drawing and writing tools

photocopies of paper frames you draw yourself

selection of magazine photos or magazines that you
deem appropriate for your class

Procedure

Talk about how people see the world—their viewpoint—and how memories
are like pictures in the mind.

Introduce cameras, explaining that the person using the camera con-
trols what the subject of the photo will be. Discuss how the children can
use a camera as a "safe window" to see things that might be too scary to
look at directly. With a camera, the child can choose to turn off a scene or
look at something different. A camera lens allows a child to view a scene
without being part of it.

Discuss what some of these imaginary scary images might be. Encourage the children to look through magazines like *National Geographic* or at
photos you have cut out to find images that are new or unusual to them.
Ask the children to use or look through the camera viewfinder and think
about how it makes them feel to see a scene but not be in it. Does it make
them feel safer, stronger, or more courageous?

Variations

Encourage the children to use their imaginations and draw private pictures of experiences or memories that are scary. Then have them draw a

second picture of how they might change that memory by looking at it through a camera. Discuss with the children how they might be able to change or create alternative memories or viewpoints without the camera by using their imaginations.

Issues
powerlessness, disconnection, loss

Purpose
To provide an opportunity for children to control what they see.

ACTIVITY 39

Heart Healer

Materials

children's book *Sofia and the Heartmender* by Marie Olofsdotter

unlined paper

drawing and writing tools

business-size envelopes

Procedure

Read *Sofia and the Heartmender.* Discuss shadow monsters and any insights the children learned from the story. Talk about whether it might be helpful for the children to create an imaginary "Heart Healer" for themselves. Encourage the children to imagine the sort of person who would make a good Heart Healer for them or another child they know in real life or from TV. What special qualities would this Heart Healer have? Are there any special tools or resources this Heart Healer would carry?

Ask them to draw the Heart Healer they have imagined.

Suggestions

Discuss the possibility of drawing Heart Healers who could bring a message of comfort and hope to children with special needs. What children might like to receive such a drawing and message? You might suggest a local children's hospital or homeless shelter. Offer envelopes to the children who want to mail their Heart Healers. Stuff, seal, and collect the envelopes. Mail these only after making arrangements with a staff person at the designated hospital or shelter.

Issues

physical or emotional insecurity, rejection, powerlessness

Purpose

To help children develop and trust their personal strengths.

ACTIVITY 40

My Transformer

Materials

chart paper and marker

unlined paper (fourteen inches by seven inches) divided in half by a line down the middle

drawing tools

Procedure

Ask the children if any of them have seen a movie or TV program about a transformer. Allow discussion, and share that it is perfectly natural to dream about having the power to transform things that scare us and turn them into heroes that could keep us safe and secure.

Invite the children to describe how a hero might help them stay safe and secure. Write their responses on chart paper.

Have each child select something scary to transform. It could be a roaring lion, a ghost, a dragon, or a monster of their own imagination. The children should draw the scary creature on the left side of their paper and the transformed hero-like creature on the right side. Discuss how the transformed image helps the group feel safe and secure.

Issues

powerlessness, hopelessness, insecurity

Purpose

To introduce to children the power of their imagination over fear, and to give children opportunities to learn the courage to face their fears.

ACTIVITY 41

Toolbox for Fixing the World

Materials
unlined paper
drawing and writing tools

Procedure

Discuss what might make the world a better place. What needs to be fixed to build a world safe for children? Encourage the children to think symbolically when considering what tools would be needed to fix the world. Make a list of tools on the blackboard. If the children need guidance, offer the following suggestions: a file to smooth the rough edges, a rubber hammer to pound out the dents, a paintbrush for a shiny new look, or a broom to sweep away yet another thing. Be sure to guide them toward constructive outcomes.

Suggestions
Have the children draw a toolbox and the tools they would select to make the world a better place for children.

Issues
hopelessness, powerlessness

Purpose
To empower children and help them build a sense of their future.

ACTIVITY 42

Tongue Depressor Puppets

Materials

tongue depressors

colored construction paper

fabric or yarn

drawing and writing tools

stapler or glue

Procedure

Do this activity as a follow-up to a book the group read together or a video they watched that has a favorable ending. Have children make tongue depressor puppets of the characters. Encourage them to create different story lines and endings for the book or video.

This activity is also good for special times when a tragic community or national event occurs, such as a fire, earthquake, or terrorist attack, and all the children are aware of it. Discuss the characters the children would like to include and the roles they would like to play. The following are some suggested characters:

- police officers
- emergency medical persons
- doctors
- nurses
- social workers
- athletes
- family members
- neighbors

- clergy
- playmates
- elected officials

Suggestions

Encourage the children to work in groups and create scripts (see chapter 9 for information on writing puppet scripts).

Issues

disempowerment, fear

Purpose

To provide opportunities for children to rework situations and create more favorable endings.

Building Dreams

Materials

construction materials such as cardboard boxes and tubes, empty spools, yarn, cotton balls, and chenille stems

glue and/or tape

Procedure

This activity can be done as a group or individually. Encourage the children to build a school, hospital, playground, or backyard of their dreams, using construction materials. Remind them to create one in which they would feel safe, happy, and successful.

Encourage them to draw pictures of any people they would like to have join them in their dream building. Have them draw pictures of what they would like the inside of the buildings to look like.

Suggestions

Encourage the children to list the activities they will do while they are in their dream building. Have them compose letters inviting anyone they wish to their dream place.

Issues

powerlessness, insecurity, loss

Purpose

To encourage children to realize the power of dreaming.

ACTIVITY
44

A Dreaming Pillowcase

Materials
unlined paper and markers
white and solid-colored pillowcases, one for each child
fabric markers

Procedure

Discuss with the children how natural it is for children—and even adults—to dream at night. Talk about how pleasant dreams are nice to have, but scary ones are disturbing and can wake us up during the night. After a scary dream, it can be hard to fall back to sleep and frustrating to sleep again if the nightmare returns.

Ask, "Have you ever thought about what might help you to have mostly pleasant dreams? Would a dreaming pillowcase be helpful? How would you decorate a dreaming pillowcase?" Allow time for children to share their ideas, then provide paper and markers and have them practice drawing on paper a sample of what they will draw on their own dreaming pillowcase. When they are satisfied with their drawings, provide the pillowcases and fabric markers.

Issues
insecurity, powerlessness

Purpose
To strengthen self-regulation, empowerment, and the sense of control.

ACTIVITY 45

Designing Cities of Hope

Materials

long length of brown art paper
drawing tools

Procedure

Have the children divide into groups of four or five to design a City of Hope together. Each group gets a section of the length of paper. Have the groups draw a city block or playground in which they would feel safe and hopeful. Encourage them to think about where they could safely play or walk. Ask them to think about who would be in their city or playground to keep children safe. Suggest they include people in their drawing.

Ask each group to present their plan to the whole group.

Issues
powerlessness, insecurity

Purpose
To empower children to think about what they need in their neighborhood to feel safe.

ACTIVITY 46

Designing a Dream House

Materials

sheets of construction paper that are fourteen inches by seven inches

drawing and writing tools

rulers

sample house plan

Procedure

Discuss the importance of dreams and the ability to think about dreams at any time. Give each child paper, drawing tools, and other materials necessary to design a dream house. Encourage the children to draw plans of a dream house that they can visit whenever they need to. Younger children can describe the floor plan for an adult to draw. They can fill in the details.

Suggestions

Talk about safe places and how everyone needs such a place. Ask the children how people know they are in a safe place. Ask them how a safe place would feel to them. Then have them look at their dream houses. Is there a safe place for them in those houses? If not, encourage the children to change their plan to include such a place.

Issues
powerlessness, insecurity, disconnection

Purpose
To empower children to think about a house where they would feel safe.

ACTIVITY 47

The Powerful Beat

Materials

recording of human heartbeats or a teddy bear designed for infants with such a recording inside

recordings or videos of various rhythmic drumming

percussion instruments

Procedure

Ask if any of the children knows why some families place a ticking clock next to their new puppies, especially at night. Explain that the ticking of the clock reminds the puppy of the sound of the mother dog's heartbeat, so the puppy does not feel as lonely.

Listen to a recording of the human heartbeat. Ask if anyone knows why recordings of heartbeats are placed into teddy bears and other baby toys. Do babies need comforting just like puppies do? Ask what feelings the children have while listening to the heartbeat.

Listen to recordings of different drum music. Ask the children how they feel when they listen to the music. Discuss their responses, and talk about when such recordings might be comforting and relaxing to hear. How do different beat speeds or tempos cause people to feel?

Introduce percussion instruments to the children, such as drums, sand blocks, maracas, or rhythm sticks. Pass out the instruments. Ask the children to demonstrate on the various instruments a beat or tempo they find comforting and relaxing. Discuss other feelings generated by percussion instruments—for both the player and the listener. For example, a fast drum beat might be exciting for the listener but eventually exhausting for the drummer.

Discuss ways the children could improvise to create a healing beat or tempo when they need it to comfort themselves. One example might be a ticking clock in their room at night or the hum of a fan.

Issues
insecurity, feeling disconnected, loneliness, loss

Purpose
To help children feel secure and connected to the people and places around them.

ACTIVITY 48

Body Language

Materials

recorded marches, dance music, or dream music

Procedure

Discuss what is meant by body language and how people can show feelings without words. Put on the music. Ask the children to move around the room in rhythm, being respectful of each other's space while the music plays. After they have warmed up, tell them you will call out a behavior or an action people do or express, and you want them to show the behavior. Instruct them to use their entire body for the movement, including their head, arms, trunk, and legs, but not to use words, sounds, or their voice at all. Allow several minutes between naming behaviors. The following are some behaviors to use:

blaming	hurting	scaring
caring	laughing	screaming
comforting	listening	singing
controlling	loving	smiling
coughing	protecting	telling
crying	punishing	threatening
hiding	resisting	yelling

Issues

limited body and impulse control, self-regulation, powerlessness

Purpose

To help children express feelings in ways other than words.

ACTIVITY 49

Silently Stepping Forward

Materials

recordings or videos of rhythmic drumming

Procedure

Ask the children to move around the room, imitating the image and behavior of the animals named. Encourage them to use their entire bodies—arms, hands, face, torso, legs, and feet. Ask that they stay quiet and communicate the suggested animal image with their bodies and their walking styles. Ask that they respect the safety and space of their classmates. Describe any animals the children may not be familiar with before the activity begins. Allow the children at least two or more minutes to fully express the symbolic walking action before calling out the next animal. Remind them to be silent, as needed.

Here are some suggested animal identities:

angry alligator	happy hippo	quarreling quail
bellowing buffalo	incredible insect	roaring raccoon
brave bear	insolent ibex	slithering snake
courageous cheetah	jolly jaguar	treacherous tiger
dancing deer	karate kangaroo	unlovable unicorn
dangerous dragon	laughing llama	vivacious vulture
elegant elk	limping leopard	wacky walrus
fierce feline	mad monster	whimpering weasel
foxy fox	nasty night owl	yelping yak
graceful giraffe	obstinate ostrich	zany zebra
	puffing panther	

After going through some of the animals, listen to the drum recordings of different tempos. Play them again, and ask the children to match an animal style with the beat or tempo being played. Repeat with different tempos as interest allows.

Issues

powerlessness, insecurity

Purpose

To help children understand and appreciate their ability to be brave and act on their own feelings.

ACTIVITY 50

The Screaming Beat

Materials

piano or drum or a recording of a drum

Procedure

Play a piano or drum or a recording of drumming, and encourage the children to move around the room, repeating their own name in beat with the music. As you increase and decrease the volume and tempo, encourage the children to match their voice volume, body movements, and energy to the sounds.

Repeat this activity, having the children use the name and sound of an animal instead of their names.

Be prepared to reinforce safety guidelines and awareness for all children. Slow the tempo and volume as needed. Provide calming comfort as needed.

Issues

powerlessness, limited impulse control

Purpose

To show children how to release energy and regain control of themselves.

ACTIVITY 51

Mr. and Ms. Body Language

Materials

recorded music of various tempos and styles

Procedure

Play music of differing tempos and styles. While the music is playing, encourage the children to think of their entire bodies as "making" similar music, sending messages into the space around them through their body language while matching their body movement to the expressions of the music.

Suggest the children imagine their bodies are magic instruments that can scribble the music's message into the spaces around them. Caution them about respecting the space and safety of each other.

Issues

powerlessness, poor body image, physical insecurity, feelings of shame

Purpose

To provide children with a healthy opportunity to validate their own bodies, feelings, and personal space.

ACTIVITY 52

Working Out Our Feelings

Materials
masking tape
plain paper plates
markers

Procedure

Before the children arrive, draw faces showing various feelings on the paper plates. Include happy, concerned, scared, angry, jealous, amused, contented, wary, loving, friendly, curious, rejected, confident, agitated, calm, frustrated, and lonely. You will need two plates for each feeling. Tape one set of plates on the wall at a height children can reach. Be sure to make enough so each participating child will have a plate.

Hand out the other set of plates randomly to the children. One at a time, have the children define and describe their feeling plate. Then have the child walk or dramatically move through the room in a style that demonstrates the feeling face. Have the children end by finding the plate on the wall that matches theirs. Be sure to applaud or otherwise affirm each child's enactment.

Issues
powerlessness, loss, physical insecurity, feelings of shame

Purpose
To support children in learning that feelings are expressed by their entire body.

Speaking Hands

Materials

Procedure

Discuss how we can communicate with our entire bodies or with our hands alone. Ask the children to pick a partner, then have them sit on the floor closely facing each other. Ask them to shake hands with their partner. Then ask them to describe how it felt. Was it warm, cold, firm, soft, energized, or relaxed?

Next, direct them to shake hands in a way that communicates confidence and then again to communicate gentleness. Ask them how they could tell which was which. What were the clues?

Ask one partner to communicate one of the following feelings by the way she uses her hands to touch her partner's hands. Have the partners reverse roles.

Here are suggested feelings to communicate:

caring
excitement
friendship
frustration
happiness
joy
loneliness
sadness
tenderness

Ask the children how they decided which way to shake or use their hands or how they could tell what feeling their partner was communicating. Repeat as desired.

Issues
insecurity, lack of trust

Purpose
To support children in learning to trust their own intuition, feelings, and bodies.

ACTIVITY 54

Moving to Music

Materials

Instrumental music without lyrics, for example, the following:

Eine Kleine Nachtmusik, first movement, by Mozart

The Carnival of the Animals by Saint-Saëns

"Maple Leaf Rag" by Scott Joplin

La Valse by Maurice Ravel

Nocturnes, "Clouds" movement, by Claude Debussy

"Voices of Spring" by Johann Strauss

Procedure

Inform the class that you will play music of different styles, tempos, beats, and rhythms. They can listen to the music for a few minutes and then allow their bodies to move in the way the music guides them. Play each type of music for five to ten minutes, depending on how much the class is enjoying it.

After the music and movements are finished, discuss how they determined which way they would move. Ask if they enjoyed the activity and if they are aware that they feel differently inside now that the activity is over.

Suggestions

This activity may be helpful if initiated when the students are stressed or having a difficult time self-regulating.

Issues

awkward movements, restrained movements, inability to relax or move freely

Purpose

To allow stressed children to feel comfortable about their bodies and movements.

Dancing Hands, Bodies, and Feet

Materials

music with a relaxing, steady beat

Procedure

Ask the children to pick a partner, then kneel facing each other. Each pair should choose who will lead first. Instruct the first leaders to make a variety of hand movements, and instruct the partners to mirror those hand movements. Remind partners not to touch or interfere with each other's movement. Start the music, and allow time for the first leaders to lead the hand motions. Stop the music, and have the children change roles. Then discuss whether this was easy or hard to do. Did it feel comfortable or uneasy leading someone? Following someone? Which was easier? Why?

Ask the children to stand up and repeat the activity but to add full

arm, head, and torso movements. Stop the music, and have the children change roles. Discuss whether they feel more in control or safe when following or leading. Ask them what helped them feel comfortable when they mirrored their partner.

Ask the children to repeat the activity, this time using their entire body for the movements, including, for example, feet and lips. Instruct the children to stay within a certain amount of space. Also remind them to respect each other's body space. Stop the music, and have the children change roles. Discuss whether they are more or less comfortable using their whole body. Is it more or less difficult to feel safe and secure when using your entire body?

Issues
physical insecurity, poor body image, lack of self-control, lack of trust

Purpose
To help children gain confidence and self-control through physically leading and following others.

ACTIVITY 56

Cradling Arms

Materials
recorded lullabies

Procedure

With the children, listen to lullabies and discuss the feelings they generate. Sing some favorites together. Ask if the children liked to be rocked when they were younger. Why? How did it make them feel? Is rocking like cradling?

Ask the children to form teams of three each. Pick three teams of three to start (nine children). Have the remaining children form a large circle around them. Ask two children from each of these three teams to form a cradle by sitting on the floor facing each other with their legs crossed in lotus position. Ask the remaining children to carefully enter their individual team cradle without stepping on anyone and to sit down inside it in a position that is comfortable for all.

Play the recording of the lullabies, and encourage the children cradling to rock gently to comfort and protect the child in the cradle. Have the children in the circle help sing the lullaby as softly and lovingly as they can as they watch.

For each round of activity, announce the scenario or type of experience the music is portraying. Here are some examples:

- A lonely child needs rocking. Encourage the "baby" in the cradle to make appropriate sound effects, such as whimpering or peeping noises.
- A baby robin is in a nest during a windstorm and needs protection.

- A puppy is feeling ill and wants to be held.
- A baby squirrel has fallen from a branch and needs comforting.

Repeat the activity with other scenarios to accommodate all the children as needed.

Issues
emotional insecurity, loss, feeling unloved, poor caregiving skills

Purpose
To help children learn to trust themselves and others by giving and receiving care.

ACTIVITY 57

Body Power

Materials

any recorded soothing music, such as Pachelbel's "Canon in D," Vivaldi's "Summer" from *The Four Seasons*, or Brahms's "Lullaby"

Procedure

Encourage children to use their hands as instruments of healing by slowly, gently moving their hands over their own bodies from head to feet without actually touching the body. Ask them to imagine they are sending themselves warm, healing energy. Encourage them to concentrate on the areas of their bodies that may especially need this healing warmth and to receive it with joy and gratitude. Allow plenty of time for the children to think, feel, and sense this activity.

Ask interested children to move close to another child and gently give this warm, healing energy to one another. Reassure those not interested in working with another child that it is good to continue on their own. Tell all the children to allow their bodies to move with the music. Discuss the activity. Ask if the children could feel the warmth by using their imaginations and if the activity helped anyone feel relaxed. (Please note this activity is a good complement to activity 55.)

Issues
powerlessness, limited impulse control

Purpose
To provide opportunities for children to send healing energy to themselves and others.

ACTIVITY 58

Gentle Touches

Materials

any recorded soothing music, such as Pachelbel's "Canon in D," Vivaldi's "Summer" from *The Four Seasons*, or Brahms's "Lullaby"

Procedure

Discuss various kinds of touches, such as uncomfortable touches and comforting touches that calm children and allow them to relax. Record the different touches so children can see the list. Explain to the children that everyone has the right to choose what kind of touch to give and receive. Affirm that everyone has the ability to make choices. At any time during this activity, be sure to allow any child not to participate.

Discuss which kinds of touches the children would like to receive, which ones they would like to share with others, and which ones they wish would never happen to anyone. Ask what kinds of emotions they feel when they receive gentle, caring touches on their arms or faces. Could giving gentle, caring touches bring those same feelings?

Invite the children to choose a partner. Have one partner sit relaxed on the floor with eyes closed. Have the other partner kneel close and gently stroke the relaxed child's face, cheeks, and neck, while very gently swaying the head in rhythm with the music. After several minutes, ask the giving children to move their hands to gently stroke the receiving children's shoulders and upper back. Ask the receiving children to be aware of the comforting warmth being given through the gentle strokes and touching. Encourage the children to freely absorb and receive the healing comfort.

After several minutes, ask the giving children to place their han[d]
their sides and feel the comforting warmth that passed between them and
their partners.

Discuss what it felt like to be the receiver of the comforting touches.
Did they feel warmth or coldness? Safe or unsafe? What did it feel like to
be the giver of the gentle strokes? Caring or uncaring? Strong or weak?
Accepted or rejected? Have the partners switch places, and repeat the
exercise and discussion.

Issues
low tolerance for risk taking, lack of trust, emotional insecurity

Purpose
To help children learn to trust themselves and others.

Giving Friendship Gifts

Materials

recorded soothing music with a steady, even tempo

Procedure

Talk about giving friendship and affection. What makes it possible for a person to give and receive gifts of friendship? How do trusting and liking yourself and being happy and worry-free fit in? Can anyone ever have too much affection or friendship? Too little?

Ask the children to choose a partner and sit on the floor, facing each other with their legs crossed, so that their knees almost touch. Play soothing music. Ask one partner in each pair to pick an imaginary, valuable gift out of the air or from behind himself and give it, gently and lovingly, to his partner. Ask the givers to "speak" only with their eyes and face and to use no words or sounds.

Encourage the receiving partners to accept the gift with delight and sincerity, demonstrating their joy through their gentle, receiving hands and glowing faces. After they have communicated this appreciation, ask the receivers to place the imaginary gift gently on the floor near them. Have the children reverse their roles and repeat the activity.

Guide the children in a discussion of their experiences and feelings. The following are some questions to ask: How did you feel as you received the gift? Did it matter that it was only an imaginary gift? What about the gift made you feel cared for and valued? How did you feel when you gave the gift? Did it bother you to give an invisible gift? Could you sense that the receiver appreciated your gift? How could you tell?

Allow the children to share the identity of the gifts, if they would like.

Issues
insecurity, loss, feeling unloved or unwanted, being uncared for

Purpose
To help children learn to trust themselves and others by giving and receiving care.

9. Healing Language Arts

Language arts provide meaningful healing opportunities for preschool, elementary, and middle school students. At the same time, language arts can expand and strengthen a school's established educational goals. By outlining specific goals and challenges for creative writing, educators can provide children with a constructive way to relieve themselves from personal stress and anxieties through fictional, symbolic characters (Steele and Malchiodi 2012).

Individual or group storytelling allows children who do not yet write or who find writing stressful to participate in creative literacy activities. Based on your familiarity with the children, assign teams where one child records the unfolding story while the other "reporters" dictate. Teacher aides or student mentors could be alternative recorders. All recorders must understand that taking dictation means asking only judgment-free questions for clarification. Young children can also draw their stories and be invited to tell about them. When working with children who have well-developed writing skills, my book *Reaching and Teaching Stressed and Anxious Learners in Grades 4–8* is a good resource.

The personal meanings behind such creative writings must remain private and confidential unless the child chooses to elaborate or share.

Creative writing assignments are never to be used to get information. It is essential for you to remember that when children are offered opportunities to explore and express their feelings, needs, and beliefs through creative writing, neither the story line nor the child should be judged or criticized. Whenever children are encouraged to disclose their personal perspectives or intuitive senses through literary activities, the philosophical or moral content must remain free of evaluation or comment. When children write their own stories, read them first before inviting children to share them with the group. Any potentially damaging or intensely private issues should not be shared.

The key to empowerment is the process, not the final literary product. Children can heal vicariously as they become connected to a character in their story, working through the same or similar experiences and feelings. You may not even be aware when or if children are using the assignment as a healing exercise. The child engaged in the cathartic process may not even be aware of it.

As indicated earlier, healing breakthroughs can get rid of accumulated negative energy. This may result in immediate behavioral changes for some children. You are encouraged to view this as a natural outcome and not a discipline issue. If acting-out behaviors become prolonged, then consider referral (see appendix A for more information about referrals).

Whenever tragic local or national events are featured extensively in the media, consider introducing one of the creative writing activities from this chapter, or create one that suits the circumstances. They can apply to natural disasters, like earthquakes and tornadoes, accidents, or deliberate acts of violence. Recognizing that anxieties may not surface for six to eight months following an ordeal, consider introducing an additional literary activity at a later time or periodically as part of the curriculum.

The cathartic potential of literary activities can be reinforced by encouraging the authors to illustrate their stories or shape them into comic books or strips.

ACTIVITY 60

Power Lists

Materials

paper and writing tools

Procedure

Discuss the idea of wish lists. Affirm with children their ability to empower themselves by choosing to have strong, helping thoughts and feelings for themselves. Have the children make lists about how they could help themselves in the following ways:

- to feel safer
- to feel hopeful
- to feel less lonely
- to feel respected
- to feel happier

This exercise needs to be judgment-free, but the children need to understand that all answers or items should not bring harm to self, others, or property.

Issues

loss, stress, loneliness, fear, powerlessness

Purpose

To help children affirm their choices and recognize their personal power.

ACTIVITY 61

Letters from the Heart

Materials
paper and writing tools

Procedure

Suggest to the children that they write letters to one or more of the following:

- a person who could be their secret friend
- their own angel
- a hero of their choice
- a person they would like to have appear in their dreams
- an animal they would like to have appear in their dreams
- an animal they would choose as their friend

Variations
Children can also dictate individual letters or a group letter.

Issues
powerlessness, physical and emotional insecurity, low self-esteem

Purpose
To help children develop hope, a sense of security, and trust.

Secret Messages

Materials

paper and writing tools

stationery and envelopes

special box—decorate it with the children!

Procedure

Provide the children with stationery. Ask them to write their answers to the following questions:

- If a bird (or a lion, wolf, or butterfly) offered to deliver a special, secret message for you, what type of bird would you choose?
- What would the message say?
- To whom or where would it be delivered?
- Would it be sung or delivered on paper?

After the answers are written, have the children decorate their stationery. Pass out the envelopes. Ask them to place their stationery in envelopes, seal them, and place the envelopes in the designated special box. Assure them that the envelopes will not be opened by anyone because an imaginary animal is guarding them and will keep them safe. Honor that promise. You can ask children with limited writing skills the questions, and they can draw pictures for answers or dictate their answers to a writer.

Issues

powerlessness, physical insecurity, loneliness, loss

Purpose

To help children develop hope, security, and trust.

ACTIVITY 63

Cuddly Cartoons

Materials

paper and writing and drawing tools

photocopies of picture frames you draw yourself (Make as many copies as you will need depending on whether you will have the children work individually or as teams.)

Procedure

Instruct the children, whether working individually or in teams, to create a cartoon strip using six of the photocopied frames. Younger children can draw wordless cartoons or draw one large, frameless mural. Suggest they create a cuddly cartoon about a baby animal that deals with any of the following issues:

- feeling lonely
- getting lost
- feeling sad about the loss of someone or something
- feeling angry
- feeling scared
- being kind and caring

Variations

Provide the first frame already completed with drawings and script, and the second frame with just the drawing. Leave the remaining frames blank for the children to complete.

Issues

insecurity, loneliness, loss, fear

Purpose

To help children develop hope by learning how to resolve problems.

ACTIVITY 64

Power Comics

Materials
paper and writing and drawing tools
laminating materials (optional)
computers or multi-touch mobile devices (optional)

Procedure

Suggest the children create six-block comic strips or cartoon booklets that include at least one of the following:

- power finders
- power thinkers
- power fixers
- power helpers
- power protectors
- power friends

Tell the children that all the cartoon characters should have powers that are positive powers. Children should have full rights to be as creative as possible as they design their power characters. Discuss the importance of writing a story that involves a constructive resolution that respects all the characters and their safety rights.

Younger children could create a group cartoon or dictate the story or words to accompany their illustrations.

Variations
Depending on your resources, bind and laminate these cartoons into permanent comic books and have an author's party.

Use an application such as Toontastic by Launchpad Toys to create digital cartoons.

Issues
powerlessness, fear, vulnerability

Purpose
To help empower children through positive thinking and caring.

ACTIVITY
65

Kid Town Commercials

Materials
paper and writing tools
video camera
editing software, such as iMovie or Movie Maker
drawing tools, if creating a cartoon
props as needed, if creating a script

Procedure

Have the children divide into journalistic teams. Explain that your role as editor will be to guide the commercial production to ensure its quality and use if arrangements have been made to share the work with other children. Instruct the teams to work together to write a script for a TV commercial or public service announcement. The script can be acted out or drawn as a cartoon commercial. Suggest the following topics:

- Inform children that they have a right to be safe.
- Inform girls that they have a right to show anger, and show how to use anger constructively.
- Inform children they have a right to say no to someone who does not respect their health or safety.
- Show how to deal constructively with put-downs.
- Inform boys that they can be sad, and show how to express it.
- Inform boys that they can be caring, and show how to express it.
- Inform children that fear is normal, and show how to use intuition to stay safe.

Suggestions

After writing the commercial, produce it. Please note that if a script is being videoed, photography releases must be on file before children can participate.

Visit a TV studio.

Issues

powerlessness, loss, insecurity, anger, sadness, fear

Purpose

To help teach children constructive skills for managing anger, sadness, powerlessness, insecurity, and fear.

Puppet Scripts

Materials

paper and writing tools

props as needed for the puppet shows

various items to make the needed puppet characters
(Puppets can be made from craft sticks, socks, and
paper bags with markers and scraps of fabric and yarn.)

Procedure

Have the children divide into teams that are a comfortable size for them
and for you. Instruct each team to work together to write or dictate and
then perform puppet scripts about one of the following story ideas:

1. A lion cub did not pay attention when his aunt, the leader of the
    pride, was giving a lesson on how to hide in the tall grass for
    safety. Now the cub doesn't know what to do or how to do it and
    has to ask directions. Whom does he ask? How does he learn
    what he needs to know? When and where does he practice? How
    does he feel at the beginning of the story and at the end?

2. A little squirrel in a family of three always gets blamed for
    whatever has gone wrong. How does this feel for her? How does
    she figure out what she might do about this? How does she
    figure out what she chooses to do and what not to do? Whom
    does she talk with about this? What advice does she give her
    younger cousin about avoiding or resolving a similar situation?

3. A little puppy feels lost and lonely and doesn't have anyone he
    can depend on. What does he do to find himself a person he can

depend on? Where does he look? Whom does he talk to? How does he decide whom to choose and whom not to choose? How does he feel at the beginning of the story and at the end?

4. A dragon is burning up with anger and cannot let off steam through her nostrils because she has a cold. How does she figure out how to release her hot, angry feelings so they won't be so uncomfortable for her? How does she do this and not hurt anyone or anything else? How does she feel at the beginning of the story and at the end?

5. A tiger cub has to figure out a way to turn fear into bravery as he deals with a crocodile. What does he say to himself to think it through? How does he build his courage? How does he decide what to do and what not to do?

6. A kitten has climbed very high into a tree and doesn't know how to get down safely. She is told by one relative to do it one way and by another relative to do it another. What kinds of directions might they have given her? How does she think through the advice and decide for herself what she can do? How does she get down? What does she decide about whom she will trust in the future when she is safely down and discussing this with her grandmother?

7. A young raccoon has just awakened from a nap and is hungry. On his way to his favorite garbage can, he hears a baby raccoon crying because he is lost, wet, and cold. The young raccoon first decides to ignore the lost baby and go on to the garbage can but then stops and turns back to help the baby. What might he have thought to himself?

How did he help the baby? Did he need any help? If so, whom did he get to help him? How did he feel about himself at the end?

8. A young rabbit has much sadness and many worries. How does she get to feel better? How does she figure out what to do? Whom does she talk with? Whom does she decide not to talk with? Why? What does she say to herself and to others? What does she do for herself to feel better? How does she feel about herself at the end? What does she decide she can do for herself so she will not feel so sad and worried in the future?

9. A puppy is separated from his mommy. While he is walking around looking for her, he discovers things that remind him of her. How does he use his imagination and the memories he discovers to lessen his sadness and his loneliness? What does he connect with his memory of how warm and safe he felt when she snuggled him? What reminded him of her smell, her voice, the sound of her tail, or the feel of her hair? How did he turn these memories into comforting feelings for himself?

10. A kitten in the house alone hears a loud, scary sound. How does the kitten feel? What does she say to herself? How does she decide to do something about her own safety? What is her safety plan? How does the kitten feel about the plan? How does the plan work? How does she feel when she has finished her plan?

11. A doll is sick and is taken to the doll hospital. How does the doll feel when he sees the rooms and equipment? What do the caring doctors and nurses do for the doll? How does he start to feel better? How does the child who loves the doll feel when he is retrieved home safe and healthy? How does the doll feel?

12. A kitten's mother has adopted a lost little bunny that wandered into their yard. How does the kitten feel when the bunny snuggles up to the kitten's mom? And when mom licks the bunny? Does the kitten feel confusion? If so, why? How does she decide to tell her mom what she was feeling? How does the mom cat respond? How do the mom and the kitten heal their differences? What happens between the kitten and the bunny?

13. A bear family—Mama, Papa, and Baby—live in the woods. One day Papa Bear packs everything he has into his suitcases, shouts, "I'm leaving," and slams the door. How does Baby Bear feel? How does Baby Bear decide what to do next? What does Baby Bear decide to do next? How does Baby Bear start to deal with his feelings? Whom does Baby Bear decide to tell his feelings to? How does this help Baby Bear?

14. A baby lamb's mother doesn't like her and doesn't pay attention to her. How does the lamb feel? What does she do to try to win acceptance by her mother? How does the lamb decide she needs to find a substitute mother? What does the lamb do to begin this process? Whom does the lamb talk to about her needs?

15. A dog wants to join a pack of dogs but is not the same color as any of the other dogs. He does not recognize or feel comfortable with any of them. Explain how he decides to introduce himself. What does he decide to say or not say? What does he decide to do or not do so the other dogs will feel more comfortable? Describe how he thinks this through for himself.

Issues
powerlessness, loss, anger, feeling rejected

Purpose
To help children learn to express and deal with feelings and to generate solutions to problems.

ACTIVITY 67

People Puppets

Materials

paper and writing tools

props as needed for the puppet shows

various items to make the needed puppet characters
(Puppets can be made from craft sticks, socks, and
paper bags with markers and scraps of fabric and yarn.)

Procedure

Use the following characters, or create ones to align with the children's
environment and culture—do not use the children's real names. Post them
where everyone can see them:

- Anxious Andy
- Cautious Cole
- Cooperative Chase
- Courageous Caroline
- Frustrated Freddie
- Hassling Hannah
- Helpful Henry
- Loving Leon
- Powerful Padma
- Precious Parker
- Protector Paige
- Tearful Trey
- Troublesome Tabatha

Encourage the children to select and write one puppet script using one of these characters to resolve the issues listed here:

- How do friends or classmates show their expectations of behaviors for the title character?
- How does the title character respond to these expectations?
- How does the title character decide to believe in himself?
- How does the title character let others know that she is proud of herself?

With guidance, younger children can make up a story and act it out with the puppets that show that both boys and girls can be unique and express themselves in many ways.

Issues

insecurity with gender or feelings

Purpose

To give children opportunities to become comfortable with gender and feelings that may not fit cultural stereotypes.

The Lonely Monster

Materials

paper and writing tools

props as needed for the puppet shows

various items to make the needed puppet characters
(Puppets can be made from craft sticks, socks, and
paper bags with markers and scraps of fabric and yarn.)

Procedure

Have the children write or dictate a story about a lonely monster without
friends who tries to make friends but is rejected.

Ask the children to describe the monster's thinking process for discovering what friends might want from him. What makes potential friends
feel uncomfortable around the monster? Describe how the monster chooses
what type of a friend to be. What can the monster do to get to know others
as friends?

Variations

Perform a puppet show of the story the children create.

Issues

loneliness, feeling rejected, powerlessness

Purpose

To help children learn to make friends.

ACTIVITY
69

Taming Nightmares

Materials

paper and writing tools

Procedure

Have the children write or tell a story about a child who has bad dreams and decides how to tame the characters in the nightmares and make them less scary.

Discuss with the children how the child decides to tame the characters. What are the possible problems? How are the dreams understood, and how does the child feel about the dream? When the child feels confident that the bad characters have been tamed, whom does the child share the experience of success with and celebrate the joy with?

Variations

Listen to the poet reading *The Adventures of Isabel* by Ogden Nash, found on YouTube. Discuss how Isabel deals with her dreams.

Issues

fear, flashbacks or nightmares, powerlessness

Purpose

To help children learn to trust in themselves and cope with their fears.

The Secret

Materials
paper and writing tools

Procedure

Have the children write an adventure story about a child who has gone to a place he was told not to go alone. While there, the child sees something happen that is so scary he decides not to tell anyone about it. Have the children describe how the child feels in body and mind. When the child returns from his adventure, he wants to forget the event, but the secret memory keeps coming back. Have the children include in their stories how the child tries to keep from remembering. They should describe the thinking process he uses to decide the secret needs to be shared: How does the child select the person to tell? How does he feel after sharing the secret?

Issues
fear from flashbacks, powerlessness

Purpose
To help children clarify their reasoning and affirm their feelings and options.

A Safety Plan

Materials
paper and writing and drawing tools

Procedure

Discuss feeling safe and feeling unsafe. How could a child know or sense when unsafe places may be near? Explain what intuition is by relating it to the common experience of feeling frightened when hearing creepy music start to play in a movie or on TV.

Have the children write, draw, or tell a story about a child who fears loud noise because it brings back a bad memory and makes the child feel that she is no longer safe. Encourage each child to describe the thinking and self-talk process that led the child to believe she was not safe. Have the children outline the words or messages the scared child says to herself to help her do something about her own safety. Have each child describe her complete safety plan, thinking about where, when, and how. Have each child describe her feelings about herself when she has created a sense of security.

Suggestions

Have the children who write the story illustrate it with a complete floor plan as part of the safety plan.

Issues
fear, powerlessness

Purpose
To empower children by helping them expand their problem-solving skills.

ACTIVITY 72

Sad Tales

Materials
paper and writing and drawing tools

Procedure

Have the children write, draw, or tell a story about a child who finds a baby kitten who is obviously not healthy and strong. Ask the students to include how the child tenderly cares for the baby kitten until it dies after a week. Encourage them to describe the child's confusion and anger over why something so small and helpless dies. What does the child say to himself? Are there any "what-ifs" he might think about? How does the child express or act out his angry feelings?

Ask the students to describe how the child decides what is anger and what is sadness and how to relieve those feelings. What does the child choose to do about his angry and sad feelings? Encourage children to include how the child chooses to share these feelings with someone he trusts. How does the child decide who that person might be? Describe any actions the child and the person he talks to may choose to do to resolve or complete the grieving process.

Issues
loss, grief

Purpose
To provide children with a way to affirm and process their feelings of loss or grief.

ACTIVITY 73

Lonesome Tales

Materials

paper and writing and drawing tools

Procedure

Have the children write, draw, or tell a story about a child who is feeling very sad because a family member the child loves is no longer a part of the family or available to the child. The child also feels bad—angry and rejected. Ask the students to include how the child feels. Because the child feels bad, she does something uncaring and hurtful. How could feeling bad lead to feeling angry and wanting to hurt something or someone? Encourage the children to explain the thinking process and what the child in the story says silently to herself. Have the children describe how the child figures out how to manage the angry feelings and release them without hurting herself, others, or property.

Issues
loss, separation, loneliness, anger

Purpose
To help children see the connection between grief and anger and recognize positive choices.

ACTIVITY 74

The Magic Trunk

Materials
paper and writing and drawing tools
puppet show supplies

Procedure

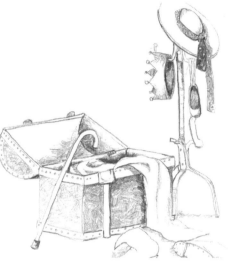

Have the children write, draw, or tell a story about a child who finds a magic trunk filled with special clothes or costumes and accessories or props. Explain to the children that on the trunk lid are directions that say, "Choose who or what you wish to be. Reach into the trunk and you will find a set of clothes that will turn you into that person." Instruct the children to pick what or whom they want the child in the story to be, choose what clothes and props are needed, and describe how the child who wears them feels. Ask the children to describe what the child will now be able to do, how the child now feels about himself, and how others around the child respond. Is the child treated differently than before? Encourage the children to give the story a positive ending.

Suggestions
Illustrate the story, or make it into a puppet script or a play.

Issues
powerlessness, fear, insecurity

Purpose
To empower children by making them aware of their choices.

A Friend in Need

Materials

paper and writing tools

Procedure

Have the children write or tell a story about a child who feels lonely and insecure and wants to be cared for in a stable environment. Ask the children to answer the questions:

- How does the child feel?
- How does the child decide she has a right to feel secure and to be cared for?
- How does the child decide she will find someone who will be a caring friend to her?

Ask the children to describe the thought process and what the child in the story said to herself. They should include how the child in the story decided where to find this caring person and how she selected the person. Have children include the very first experience these two characters shared together and how the child felt. Ask them to describe how the child is looking forward to the future now that there is more stability and caring in her life.

Issues

insecurity, loneliness, loss

Purpose

To help children learn alternative sources for caring and stability.

ACTIVITY 76

Comfort Zones

Materials

paper and writing and drawing tools

Procedure

Have the children write, draw, or tell a story about a child who has just transferred to a new school and is finding the experience stressful and lonely. Ask the children to describe how the child feels. Is it hard to go to the new place each morning? Provide a scenario by describing how the child tries to make friends with a group of children at lunch and he is rejected and made fun of. Then ask the children to describe how the child in the story deals with this and finds another place to sit.

Children should continue the story by explaining how the child feels as he goes home and begins to daydream about his dream school or center.

- What is the child's dream school or center like?
- How do the adults and children treat new children?
- What might they say and do differently?
- Is there one place in the dream school or center where the child feels especially safe and comfortable?
- Who else might come to that place?
- What does the child think about and say to himself to make it possible for him to feel comfortable about returning the next day?

Issues

stress, fear, insecurity, loss

Purpose

To help children manage their stress and fears while building a sense of security.

ACTIVITY 77

Broken Wing, Broken Dreams

Materials
paper and writing and drawing tools

Procedure

Have the children write, draw, or tell a story about a child who finds a hawk or pigeon with a broken wing. (Please note, children who tend to have behavior outbursts usually relate well to the wild spirit of a hawk.)

Ask the children to describe how the child decides to help the injured bird. They can use the following questions to guide their story:

- What are the bird's reactions to the child's approach and handling?
- How does the child feel while trying to help the bird?
- How will the child care for the bird?
- What specific things does she do for the bird?
- Why does she do these things?
- What might the child say to herself as she provides care and comfort for the bird?
- How do her family and friends respond to the bird and the child's caring for it?
- How does the child feel about their responses?
- What does she say to herself about their responses?
- How does the bird respond to the child as the care and healing progress?
- How does the child feel as this is happening?
- How does the story end?
- What happens to the bird?
- How does the child feel about the outcome for herself and the bird?

Suggestions

Contact your local department of natural resources to learn who in the area is licensed to care for injured wild animals. Arrange, if possible, to have them bring an injured bird or other small animal to your classroom.

Issues

loneliness, loss, hopelessness

Purpose

To affirm needs for hope and a future, and to honor the strengths of free spirits.

Star Bright, Star Power

Materials
paper and writing and drawing tools

Procedure

Have the children write, draw, or tell a bedtime story about a child who finds great comfort in looking at his own special star at night through the window near his bed. Ask the children to describe what the special star looks like and the way it sparkles. Here are questions to guide their work about the light from the star coming through the window into the bedroom:

- How does the child know which star of the millions in the sky is her special star?
- What are the star's special qualities, such as its colors or temperature?
- What does the star do for the child?
- What is the child's relationship with the star?
- How does the child talk with or send messages to the star?

- How does the child decide what she wants or needs from the star?
- How does the child feel as the starlight wraps around her?
- What can the child now do, thanks to the special strength the star has given her?

Issues
powerlessness, loneliness

Purpose
To help children develop their self-empowerment skills.

Appendix A

Making Referrals

The symbolic healing activities offered in this book are not intended to be a substitute for the range of community mental health services available to children through many public and private systems. Nor are they to be used as a substitute for reporting suspected child abuse to the appropriate local authorities. All educators and caregivers are mandated to report suspected child abuse.

This book is offered as a practical guide for adults who want to provide children with active ways to integrate their life experiences with their experiences in schools, centers, or any other group settings. The activities are designed to help empower children and give them hope for their future.

The healing activities presented in this book can be used as reinforcement for children who might be receiving community mental health services. The introduction of a healing exercise may alert you to a child who appears to need referral to professional mental health services.

The decision by a teacher or caregiver to make a referral is usually the culmination of a caring, introspective evaluation. To refer a child for mental health services is as much a part of any comprehensive educational program as arranging for a math or reading tutor. It is the sign of an insightful adult who respects and cares for children.

How to Tell If a Child Needs to Be Referred
- The child is so depressed or withdrawn that participation in regular classroom, program, or playground activities is no longer possible.
- The child has become highly aggressive or outbursts are so intense that the safety of the child or others is at risk.
- The child has spoken or written of suicidal behavior or other intentions to harm himself.
- The child reports having heard voices or seen things others are unable to validate.

What You Can Do to Help

- Develop a trusting relationship with a child's parent(s) or guardian(s) to learn what their insights are into possible reasons for the child's behaviors and experiences. These might include household moves, fires, the loss of a pet, the loss of an important adult relationship, a new sibling, a change in the health of a family member, or economic changes.

- Become familiar with the local agencies that provide services for children and their families.

- Keep a behavioral log that records the specific dates and types of troubling behavior. This log may strengthen your recommendation for referral and provide significant information for the eventual service provider.

- Inform the parent(s) or guardian(s) of your observations and concerns, even in cases of suspected child abuse.

- Inquire if the child is now receiving or ever has received counseling and if the parent(s) or guardian(s) have any preferred agencies.

- Honor the confidentiality of the child and family when securing services for a child.

- Allow the parent(s) or guardian(s) to initiate services with the agency of their choice.

- Allow the parent(s) or guardian(s) to set the date for the next appointment with you as a continuation of your support for them.

- Your success in encouraging the parent(s) or guardian(s) to carry through on the referral is crucial to the process. Offer to walk the parent(s) through the process. Explain what it will mean for them. Tell them how you can help and support them. Your relationship with them will be a vital part of securing the needed services for the child.

- Your commitment to the child's long-term well-being may be your best ally in working with the parent(s) or guardian(s). It will also be your finest professional characteristic.

- If you sense it would be welcomed, form a team with another staff member who also has a trusting relationship with the child and parent(s) to reinforce your efforts to support the family.

Making referrals can be frightening for adults. Others may discourage you by saying you are overreacting. It is essential that you follow your thoughtful observation and strong intuitions based on your relationship with the child to follow through in every way necessary to get the help the child needs. You may be the person who literally saves the child's life, physically or psychologically. Empower yourself, and do what needs to be done!

Appendix B: Resources

Chapter 2

Resources for Teachers Guiding Students through Trauma

ChildTrauma Academy

www.childtrauma.org

The ChildTrauma Academy (CTA) seeks to improve the lives of traumatized and mistreated children by providing resources to organizations and individuals who wish to ameliorate the circumstances of children who may be at high risk. CTA offers and encourages education, training, and direct service.

The National Child Traumatic Stress Network

www.NCTSN.org

The National Child Traumatic Stress Network (NCTSN) strives to change the course of traumatized children's lives through their direct care. The NCTSN was established by Congress in 2000 and seeks to increase awareness of communities about America's traumatized youth, providing them with access to programs, services, research, and education.

The National Institute for Trauma and Loss in Children

www.starrtraining.org/trauma-and-children

The National Institute for Trauma and Loss in Children (TLC) works with families, educators, child care professionals, and trauma professionals to establish environments where traumatized children can prosper. TLC provides training programs, interventions, and education to better the lives of children who have experienced trauma.

Pet Partners

www.petpartners.org

Pet Partners is a resource that wishes to demonstrate that physical, emotional, and psychological lives can be improved by positive interactions between humans and animals. By providing a therapy animal program, education, research, and other resources, Pet Partners is a tool that can be used to improve an individual's health and well-being.

Therapy Dogs International
www.tdi-dog.org
Therapy Dogs International (TDI) provides nursing homes, hospitals, or other places where therapy dogs are needed with volunteer handlers and their therapy dogs. TDI wishes to increase awareness about the benefits that therapy dogs can provide for individuals who need comfort or enjoyment.

Children's Books about Fear and Trauma

Sandy's Suitcase by Elsy Edwards*
A Terrible Thing Happened by Margaret M. Holmes
Beautiful Dragons and Other Fears: A Workbook for Children by Joy
    Johnson
*Stately Queens and Shining Knights: A Resource for Parents and
    Caregivers Helping Children Experiencing Fear* by Joy Johnson,
    Andrea Gambill, and Diane Ferrara
Brave Bart: A Story for Traumatized and Grieving Children by Caroline
    H. Sheppard*

Chapter 3

Resources for Teachers Addressing Bullying

Peace Education Foundation
www.PeaceEducation.org
The Peace Education Foundation works closely with children and their families to promote peace in their communities. By providing them with training, workshops, research, and educational resources, the Peace Education Foundation aims to spread peacemaking skills throughout the world.

*The Peaceful Classroom: 162 Easy Activities to Teach Preschoolers
    Compassion and Cooperation* by Charles A. Smith
This book is written for preschool teachers but can be used by early elementary teachers as well—simply adjust the activities to match the needs of the children.

---

* These books are no longer in print; however, they are excellent resources if you can find them in your community library or from a used-book seller.

Children's Books about Bullying

Personal Space Camp by Julia Cook
My Secret Bully by Trudy Ludwig
Say Something by Peggy Moss

Chapter 5

Resources for Teachers for Understanding Grief

Helping the Grieving Student: A Guide for Teachers by The Dougy Center
This book provides teachers of all school ages with a helpful guide to dealing with grieving students in the classroom.

Grief Comes to Class: An Educator's Guide by Majel Gliko-Braden
Written by a teacher and school counselor, this book aids educators and parents in providing comfort and supportive care to a child in a classroom setting following a death experience.

Lifetimes: The Beautiful Way to Explain Death to Children by Bryan
    Mellonie and Robert Ingpen
Lifetimes provides children with a practical, illustrated explanation of the lifetimes of various living things, including plants, animals, and humans. This book explains in a caring, simple manner how death is a natural part of life.

Children's Books about Losing a Pet

Saying Goodbye to Lulu by Corinne Demas
*Ragtail Remembers: A Story That Helps Children Understand Feelings of
    Grief* by Liz Duckworth
*Zach and His Dog: A Story of Bonding, Love, and Loss for Children and
    Adults to Share Together* by David K. Meagher*
The Tenth Good Thing about Barney by Judith Viorst
Harry & Hopper by Margaret Wild

* This book is no longer in print; however, it is an excellent resource if you can find it in your community library or from a used-book seller.

Children's Books about Grieving

I Know I Made It Happen: A Gentle Book about Feelings by Lynn Bennett Blackburn

Grief Is Like a Snowflake by Julia Cook

The Life of Bud by Laura W. Eckroat

Aarvy Aardvark Finds Hope: A Read Aloud Story for People of All Ages about Loving and Losing, Friendship and Hope by Donna O'Toole

Tear Soup: A Recipe for Healing after Loss by Pat Schwiebert and Chuck DeKlyen

Children's Books about New Siblings

Bye-Bye, Baby! by Richard Morris

One Special Day: A Story for Big Brothers and Sisters by Lola M. Schaefer

Children's Books about Moving

Billy Had to Move: A Foster Care Story by Theresa Ann Fraser

Moving Is Hard by Joan Singleton Prestine*

Shadow Moves: A Story for Families and Children Experiencing a Difficult or Traumatic Move by Caroline H. Sheppard*

Children's Books about Change in School

Disappearing Desmond by Anna Alter

The Class in Room 44: When a Classmate Dies by Lynn Bennett Blackburn

Children's Books about Illness

Chester Raccoon and the Acorn Full of Memories by Audrey Penn

What's Happening to Grandpa? by Maria Shriver

* These books are no longer in print; however, they are excellent resources if you can find them in your community library or from a used-book seller.

Children's Books about Changes in a Family

Everett Anderson's Goodbye by Lucille Clifton
The "D" Word: Divorce by Julia Cook
At Daddy's on Saturdays by Linda Walvoord Girard
Grandpa's Soup by Eiko Kadono
The Brightest Star by Kathleen Maresh Hemery*
I Don't Want to Talk about It by Jeanie Franz Ransom

Children's Books about Violence

Why Did It Happen? Helping Children Cope in a Violent World by Janice Cohn*
The Pout-Pout Fish in the Big-Big Dark by Deborah Diesen
A Safe Place to Live: A Story for Children Who Have Experienced Domestic Violence by Michelle A. Harrison*
When They Fight by Kathryn White

Children's Books about Self-Worth

You've Got Dragons by Kathryn Cave
Glenna's Seeds by Nancy Edwards
Sofia and the Heartmender by Marie Olofsdotter
Steps and Stones: An Anh's Anger Story by Gail Silver
Finding the Green Stone by Alice Walker*

---

* These books are no longer in print; however, they are excellent resources if you can find them in your community library or from a used-book seller.

Appendix C: Index of Activities by Issue

Activity	Anger	Anxiety	Confusion	Disconnect	Disempowerment	Distrust	Fear	Feeling	Grief	Hopelessness	Hurt	Insecurity	Lack of self-control, trust, empowerment	Limited body control	Limited impulse control	Loneliness	Loss	Low self-esteem	Low tolerance for risk taking	Need	Poor body image	Poor caregiving skills	Poor problem-solving skills	Powerlessness	Rejection	Sadness	Separation	Shame	Stress	Unexpressed feelings	Vulnerability
Bad–Dream Catcher #33												•												•							
Becoming a Helper Friend #12																									•						
Bells of Courage #17												•								•											
Big and Little Lions #11																				•											•
Body Language #48														•	•									•							
Body Power #57															•									•							
Broken Wing, Broken Dreams #77										•						•	•														
Building Dreams #43												•					•							•							

203

Activity	Anger	Anxiety	Confusion	Disconnect	Disempowerment	Distrust	Fear	Feeling	Grief	Hopelessness	Hurt	Insecurity	Lack of self-control, trust, empowerment	Limited body control	Limited impulse control	Loneliness	Loss	Low self-esteem	Low tolerance for risk taking	Need	Poor body image	Poor caregiving skills	Poor problem-solving skills	Powerlessness	Rejection	Sadness	Separation	Shame	Stress	Unexpressed feelings	Vulnerability
Care Wrapping #8												•								•											
Caring Blanket #36							•					•				•															
Caring Coupons #26								•	•																						
Color Out All of the Anger and Sadness #23	•															•	•							•		•					
Coloring Feelings #19																														•	
Coloring Solutions #24										•												•	•								
Comfort Zones #76							•					•				•													•		
Cradling Arms #56								•				•				•						•									
Cuddly Cartoons #63							•					•				•	•														

Activity	Anger	Anxiety	Confusion	Disconnect	Disempowerment	Distrust	Fear	Feeling	Grief	Hopelessness	Hurt	Insecurity	Lack of self-control, trust, empowerment	Limited body control	Limited impulse control	Loneliness	Loss	Low self-esteem	Low tolerance for risk taking	Need	Poor body image	Poor caregiving skills	Poor problem-solving skills	Powerlessness	Rejection	Sadness	Separation	Shame	Stress	Unexpressed feelings	Vulnerability
Dancing Hands, Bodies, and Feet #55												•	•								•										
Designing a Dream House #46												•												•			•				
Designing Cities of Hope #45												•												•							
Drawings for Power #20																	•							•							
Dream Family #34													•														•				
Dreaming Pillowcase #44												•												•							
Flubber #6												•																	•		
Friend in Need #75												•				•	•														
Gentle Touches #58												•	•						•												

Activity	Anger	Anxiety	Confusion	Disconnect	Disempowerment	Distrust	Fear	Feeling	Grief	Hopelessness	Hurt	Insecurity	Lack of self-control, trust, empowerment	Limited body control	Limited impulse control	Loneliness	Loss	Low self-esteem	Low tolerance for risk taking	Need	Poor body image	Poor caregiving skills	Poor problem-solving skills	Powerlessness	Rejection	Sadness	Separation	Shame	Stress	Unexpressed feelings	Vulnerability
Giving Friendship Gifts #59								•				•					•														
Growing Empathy #10						•						•			•																
Hands of Courage #14												•								•											
Healing Garden #32		•									•	•					•														
Heart Healer #39												•												•	•						
Hide and Find #3												•					•										•				
Kid Town Commercials #65	•					•						•					•							•	•						
Letters from the Heart #61												•								•				•							
Lonely Monster #68																•								•	•						

Activity	Anger	Anxiety	Confusion	Disconnect	Disempowerment	Distrust	Fear	Feeling	Grief	Hopelessness	Hurt	Insecurity	Lack of self-control, trust, empowerment	Limited body control	Limited impulse control	Loneliness	Loss	Low self-esteem	Low tolerance for risk taking	Need	Poor body image	Poor caregiving skills	Poor problem-solving skills	Powerlessness	Rejection	Sadness	Separation	Shame	Stress	Unexpressed feelings	Vulnerability
Lonely Puppy #5												•																			
Lonesome Tales #73	•															•	•										•				
Love Bank #35				•				•				•					•														
Magic Camera #38				•													•							•							
Magic Trunk #74							•					•												•							
Magic Wands of Courage #13							•													•											
Meeting Nightmares #15							•																								
Memory Chains #25				•																•											
Mother Hens #9												•								•											

Activity	Anger	Anxiety	Confusion	Disconnect	Disempowerment	Distrust	Fear	Feeling	Grief	Hopelessness	Hurt	Insecurity	Lack of self-control, trust, empowerment	Limited body control	Limited impulse control	Loneliness	Loss	Low self-esteem	Low tolerance for risk taking	Need	Poor body image	Poor caregiving skills	Poor problem-solving skills	Powerlessness	Rejection	Sadness	Separation	Shame	Stress	Unexpressed feelings	Vulnerability
Moving to Music #54														•																	
Mr. and Ms. Body Language #51												•												•				•			
My Own Hero #31				•								•												•							
My Transformer #40										•		•												•							
People Puppets #67							•					•																			
Portraits of Loving Memorials #27									•								•										•				
Portraits of Trust and Friendship #28				•					•																						
Power Comics #64							•																	•							•
Power Hats #37		•					•					•					•							•							

Activity	Anger	Anxiety	Confusion	Disconnect	Disempowerment	Distrust	Fear	Feeling	Grief	Hopelessness	Hurt	Insecurity	Lack of self-control, trust, empowerment	Limited body control	Limited impulse control	Loneliness	Loss	Low self-esteem	Low tolerance for risk taking	Need	Poor body image	Poor caregiving skills	Poor problem-solving skills	Powerlessness	Rejection	Sadness	Separation	Shame	Stress	Unexpressed feelings	Vulnerability
Power Lists #60							•									•	•							•					•		
Powerful Beat #47				•								•				•	•														
Puppet Scripts #66	•																•							•	•						
Releasing Worries and Fears #18																	•							•							
Rescue Teams #7												•								•											
Sad Tales #72									•								•														
Safety Badge #29												•					•														
Safety Plan #71				•																				•							
Safety Shields #30												•					•														

Activity	Anger	Anxiety	Confusion	Disconnect	Disempowerment	Distrust	Fear	Feeling	Grief	Hopelessness	Hurt	Insecurity	Lack of self-control, trust, empowerment	Limited body control	Limited impulse control	Loneliness	Loss	Low self-esteem	Low tolerance for risk taking	Need	Poor body image	Poor caregiving skills	Poor problem-solving skills	Powerlessness	Rejection	Sadness	Separation	Shame	Stress	Unexpressed feelings	Vulnerability
Screaming Beat #50															•									•							
Secret #70						•																		•							
Secret Messages #62												•				•	•							•							
Seeing the World through Colored Glasses #4												•			•																
Silently Stepping Forward #49												•												•							
Speaking Hands #53												•	•																		
Star Bright, Star Power #78																•								•							
Taming Nightmares #69						•																		•							

Activity	Anger	Anxiety	Confusion	Disconnect	Disempowerment	Distrust	Fear	Feeling	Grief	Hopelessness	Hurt	Insecurity	Lack of self-control, trust, empowerment	Limited body control	Limited impulse control	Loneliness	Loss	Low self-esteem	Low tolerance for risk taking	Need	Poor body image	Poor caregiving skills	Poor problem-solving skills	Powerlessness	Rejection	Sadness	Separation	Shame	Stress	Unexpressed feelings	Vulnerability
Teardrops of My Heart #21												•				•	•								•						
Tell the Telephone #1												•					•			•							•				
Tongue Depressor Puppets #42					•		•																								
Toolbox for Fixing the World #41										•														•							
Walking Bravely #16												•								•											
Wish Box #2												•					•			•							•				
Wishing Rainbow #22										•							•							•							
Working Out Our Feelings #52												•					•							•				•			

References

American Psychological Association Zero Tolerance Task Force. 2008. "Are Zero Tolerance Policies Effective in the Schools? An Evidentiary Review and Recommendations." *American Psychologist* 63 (9): 852–62. doi: 10.1037/0003-066X.63.9.852.

Amstutz, Lorraine Stutzman, and Judy H. Mullet. 2005. *The Little Book of Restorative Discipline for Schools.* Intercourse, PA: Good Books.

Badenoch, Bonnie. 2008. *Being a Brain-Wise Therapist: A Practical Guide to Interpersonal Neurobiology.* New York: W. W. Norton & Co.

Bailey, Becky A. 2000. *I Love You Rituals.* New York: Quill.

——. 2011. *Managing Emotional Mayhem: The Five Steps for Self-Regulation.* Oviedo, FL: Loving Guidance.

Brendtro, Larry K., Martin L. Mitchell, and Herman J. McCall. 2009. *Deep Brain Learning: Pathways to Potential with Challenging Youth.* Albion, MI: Starr Commonwealth.

Cohen, Barry M., Mary-Michola Barnes, and Anita B. Rankin. 1995. *Managing Traumatic Stress through Art: Drawing from the Center.* Baltimore: Sidran Press.

Cozolino, Louis. 2006. *The Neuroscience of Human Relationships: Attachment and the Developing Social Brain.* New York: W. W. Norton & Co.

——. 2013. *The Social Neuroscience of Education: Optimizing Attachment and Learning in the Classroom.* New York: W. W. Norton & Co.

Dougy Center. 1999. *35 Ways to Help a Grieving Child.* Portland, OR: The Dougy Center for Grieving Children.

Drake, Kim, Jay Belsky, and R. M. Pasco Fearon. 2013. "From Early Attachment to Engagement with Learning in School: The Role of Self-Regulation and Persistence." *Developmental Psychology,* May 6. doi: 10.1037/a0032779.

Duckworth, Angela L., and Martin E. P. Seligman. 2005. "Self-Discipline Outdoes IQ in Predicting Academic Performance of Adolescents." *Psychological Science* 16 (12): 939–44. www.sas.upenn.edu/~duckwort/images/PsychologicalScienceDec2005.pdf.

Fogarty, James A. 2000. *The Magical Thoughts of Grieving Children: Treating Children with Complicated Mourning and Advice for Parents.* Amityville, NY: Baywood Publishing Company.

Forbes, Heather T., and B. Bryan Post. 2006. *Beyond Consequences, Logic, and Control: A Love-Based Approach to Helping Children with Severe Behaviors.* Orlando, FL: Beyond Consequences Institute.

Geddes, Heather. 2006. *Attachment in the Classroom: The Links between Children's Early Experience, Emotional Well-Being and Performance in School.* London: Worth Publishing.

Gil, Eliana. 1991. *The Healing Power of Play: Working with Abused Children*. New York: The Guilford Press.

Grille, Robin. 2005. *Parenting for a Peaceful World*. New South Wales, Australia: Longueville Media.

Kagan, Richard. 2004. *Rebuilding Attachments with Traumatized Children: Healing from Losses, Violence, Abuse, and Neglect*. Binghamton, NY: Haworth Maltreatment and Trauma Press.

Levine, Peter A., and Maggie Kline. 2007. *Trauma through a Child's Eyes: Awakening the Ordinary Miracle of Healing*. Berkeley, CA: North Atlantic Books; Lyons, CO: ERGOS Institute Press.

Lovre, Cheri. 2006. *The Safe Room: A Guide for School Crisis Responders*. Bloomington, IN: Solution Tree.

Ogden, Pat. 2009. "Emotion, Mindfulness, and Movement: Expanding the Regulatory Boundaries of the Window of Affect Tolerance." In *The Healing Power of Emotion: Affective Neuroscience, Development, and Clinical Practice*, edited by Diane Fosha, Daniel J. Siegel, and Marion F. Solomon, 204–31. New York: W. W. Norton & Co.

Perry, Bruce D. 2004. Series #1: *Understanding Traumatized and Maltreated Children: The Core Concepts*. DVD. Houston, TX: The ChildTrauma Academy.

Perry, Bruce D., and Maia Szalavitz. 2006. *The Boy Who Was Raised as a Dog: And Other Stories from a Child Psychiatrist's Notebook: What Traumatized Children Can Teach Us about Loss, Love, and Healing*. New York: Basic Books.

Rothschild, Babette. 2000. *The Body Remembers: The Psychophysiology of Trauma and Trauma Treatment*. New York: W. W. Norton & Co.

Schore, Allan N. 2003. "Early Relational Trauma, Disorganized Attachment, and the Development of a Predisposition to Violence." In *Healing Trauma: Attachment, Mind, Body, and Brain*, ed. Marion F. Solomon and Daniel J. Siegel, 107–67. New York: W. W. Norton & Co.

———. 2009. "Right Brain Affect Regulation: An Essential Mechanism of Development, Trauma, Dissociation, and Psychotherapy." In *The Healing Power of Emotion: Affective Neuroscience, Development, and Clinical Practice*, ed. Diana Fosha, Daniel J. Siegel, and Marion F. Solomon, 112–44. New York: W. W. Norton & Co.

Sparks, Sarah D. 2012. "Research Traces Impact of Childhood Adversity." *Education Week*, November. www.edweek.org/ew/articles/2012/11/07/11poverty_ep.h32.html.

Steele, William, and Cathy A. Malchiodi. 2012. *Trauma-Informed Practices with Children and Adolescents*. New York: Routledge.

Szalavitz, Maia, and Bruce D. Perry. 2010. *Born for Love: Why Empathy Is Essential—and Endangered*. New York: HarperCollins.

Tronick, Edward, Als Heidelise, Lauren Adamson, Susan Wise, and T. Berry Brazelton. 1978. "The Infant's Response to Entrapment between Contradictory Messages in Face-to-Face Interaction." *Journal of the American Academy of Child Psychiatry* 17 (1): 1–13. doi:10.1016/S0002-7138(09)62273-1.

Vrtička, Pascal, and Patrik Vuilleumier. 2012. "Neuroscience of Human Social Interactions and Adult Attachment Style." *Frontiers in Human Neuroscience*, July 17. doi: 10.3389/fnhum.2012.00212.